1

Table Of Contents

Whispers of Bastet: The Magical History of Cats

Dedication

To the countless cats, both mortal and divine, who graced the land of the Pharaohs with their presence, their grace, and their enigmatic power. This work is a humble attempt to capture a fragment of their enduring legacy, to unravel the threads of their mysterious connection to the human heart and the unseen world. May their whispers continue to echo through time, reminding us of the profound and enduring bond between humanity and the feline realm. It is dedicated, too, to those scholars who have dedicated their lives to uncovering the rich tapestry of ancient Egyptian history, and to those who are inspired to delve into the mysteries that still remain. May their curiosity and dedication serve as a beacon for future generations.

Preface

For centuries, the enigmatic allure of ancient Egypt has captivated imaginations worldwide. Pyramids piercing the desert sky, hieroglyphs whispering secrets from the past, and gods and goddesses embodying the forces of nature – all contribute to the land's enduring mystique. Yet, within this rich tapestry of pharaohs, deities, and monuments, there exists a subtle, persistent thread that deserves deeper examination: the profound veneration of the cat. Far from a mere domestic animal, the cat in ancient Egypt held a sacred status, embodying divine power and embodying a mysterious connection to the unseen realms.

This book, "Whispers of Bastet," ventures into this captivating world. It is not merely a historical account, but a journey of discovery, weaving together archaeological evidence, ancient texts, and captivating narratives to illuminate the multifaceted relationship between ancient Egyptians and their feline companions. Through meticulous research and insightful analysis, we will unravel the reasons behind this profound reverence, exploring the roles cats played in mythology, religious rituals, magical practices, and even in the realm of the afterlife.

The narrative unfolds across various chapters, each delving into a unique facet of the cat's significance in ancient Egyptian civilization. From the earliest evidence of human-feline interaction to the decline of cat worship in later periods, we will uncover a rich tapestry of beliefs and practices. We will examine the iconic goddess Bastet, explore the artistry that immortalized cats in tombs and temples, and analyze the magical properties attributed to these enigmatic creatures. The journey promises to be one of wonder, discovery, and a deeper appreciation for the profound bond that existed between humanity and the feline world in ancient Egypt. Prepare to be captivated by the whispers of Bastet, and the ancient secrets they reveal.

Introduction

Ancient Egypt, a civilization renowned for its monumental architecture, intricate hieroglyphs, and complex religious beliefs, holds many captivating mysteries. Among these, the profound reverence for cats stands out as a particularly enigmatic and fascinating aspect. Unlike other cultures that might have viewed cats with suspicion or ambivalence, the ancient Egyptians elevated these graceful creatures to the status of divine beings, integrating them deeply into their religious beliefs, artistic expressions, and daily lives.

This book seeks to unveil the layers of this unique relationship, moving beyond simplistic notions of mere affection to explore the deeper spiritual, cultural, and social significance of cats within ancient Egyptian society. We will traverse the span of Egyptian history, from the earliest evidence of human-feline interaction in the Predynastic period to the waning years of the civilization under Roman rule. Along the way, we will examine a wealth of primary and secondary sources, including archaeological discoveries, artistic representations, ancient texts, and scholarly interpretations.

The narrative will focus not only on the goddess Bastet, the most prominent feline deity, but also on the broader cultural significance of cats, including their roles in mythology, religious rituals, funerary practices, magic, and medicine. We will delve into the intricate symbolism associated with cats, unraveling the complex meanings embedded in their depictions in tomb paintings, sculptures, amulets, and other artifacts. We will investigate the extraordinary phenomenon of mass cat mummification, exploring the motivations behind this practice and what it reveals about ancient Egyptian beliefs concerning the afterlife. The aim is not only to reconstruct the historical reality of the ancient Egyptian cat cult but also to interpret its significance within the broader context of ancient Egyptian religious beliefs and worldview.

The journey through these "Whispers of Bastet" promises a rich and rewarding experience, enriching our understanding of this ancient civilization and its profound connection to the feline world.

Early Evidence of Human Feline Interaction

Chapter One

The precise moment when the bond between humans and cats solidified in ancient Egypt remains shrouded in the mists of prehistory, a challenge for even the most meticulous of Egyptologists. Unlike the more readily traceable domestication of dogs, the evidence for the human-feline partnership in ancient Egypt is fragmented, requiring careful piecing together of disparate clues from archaeological digs, artistic representations, and the subtle hints embedded within ancient texts. However, by examining the available evidence, we can begin to reconstruct a plausible narrative of this pivotal moment in both human and feline history.

One of the earliest and most compelling lines of evidence comes from the analysis of skeletal remains. While the identification of unequivocally domesticated cat remains from the very earliest periods is difficult, the presence of feline skeletons in human settlements, particularly those dating to the

Neolithic period (approximately 6500-4000 BCE) and the subsequent Predynastic period (circa 4000-3100 BCE), is highly suggestive. These finds, often uncovered in close proximity to human burials or within the structures of settlements, imply a level of coexistence and possibly even a degree of integration into human life. Further research analyzing isotopic ratios within the cat bones holds the potential to clarify the feline diet, revealing whether these cats were primarily hunting independently or relying on food sources provided by humans – a key indicator of domestication.

The analysis of skeletal remains, however, offers only a limited perspective. To fully understand the nature of the early human-feline relationship, we must turn to the rich tapestry of ancient Egyptian art. While the earliest representations are stylized and less realistic, the presence of feline imagery on pottery shards, and even some tentative depictions in cave art, hints at an early recognition and possibly reverence for felines. The precise interpretation of these early images remains a matter of ongoing scholarly debate. Some scholars argue that these depictions might represent wild cats, integral to the hunter-gatherer lifestyle of the time, while others suggest a possible symbolic or even spiritual association with felines that pre-dates explicit domestication. These early artistic representations, despite their ambiguity, are invaluable clues in understanding the developing relationship between humans and cats.

The geographic distribution of the early evidence is another crucial aspect of our investigation. While evidence of early human-feline interaction appears throughout Upper and Lower Egypt, certain regions may have witnessed more intense interaction than others. Mapping the locations of feline skeletal finds and the distribution of early feline-themed artistic representations provides a spatial context for understanding the initial centers of human-feline interaction. This geographic mapping may reveal patterns suggesting the presence of early domesticated cat populations in specific areas, possibly reflecting factors like ecological conditions favorable to both humans and cats, or the concentration of human settlements that might have fostered closer contact. Detailed study of the distribution is still in its early stages but holds the promise of revealing valuable insights.

Furthermore, the study of Predynastic cemeteries offers additional compelling evidence. While the clear association of cats with human burials is primarily a phenomenon of later periods, the discovery of feline remains in some Predynastic cemeteries indicates a growing connection between humans and cats, even in death. While it is difficult to ascertain whether these interments were intentional or simply a result of cats' proximity to human settlements, their presence in these sacred spaces hints at the growing significance of cats within the broader

social and perhaps spiritual context of Predynastic Egypt. Further examination of burial practices and grave goods associated with these feline remains could offer more definite clues regarding the development of the sacred status of cats in ancient Egyptian culture.

The potential reasons for the initial human-feline interaction are numerous and interconnected. While the precise sequence of events remains debated, the mutual benefits are clear. For humans, the control of vermin, particularly rodents that threatened stored grain and posed health risks, was a significant advantage. Cats, with their innate hunting abilities, provided a natural and effective solution to this problem. This practical benefit likely played a key role in the initial stages of the relationship, fostering a level of tolerance and co-existence that ultimately led to domestication.

From the feline perspective, the proximity to human settlements offered access to a readily available food source – the leftovers from human meals – supplemented by the abundance of rodents attracted to human settlements. This beneficial co-existence, in turn, paved the way for a more profound connection over time. The initial stages involved a pragmatic collaboration that evolved into a deeply spiritual and culturally interwoven relationship that would define the cultural landscape of ancient Egypt for millennia. Further research, employing advanced techniques like DNA analysis and more sophisticated isotopic studies, promises to shed further light on the precise trajectory of this transformation, but the initial evidence clearly points toward a mutually beneficial relationship that, in time, transformed from simple co-existence to profound reverence. The whispers of this early connection continue to resonate through the archaeological record, urging further investigation to fully unveil the complex interplay between humans and cats that shaped the ancient Egyptian world. Understanding these early beginnings is crucial to appreciating the deep cultural and spiritual significance that cats attained in later periods. The transition from practical collaboration to sacred veneration represents a remarkable journey in interspecies relations, one that continues to fascinate and inspire scholars and cat lovers alike.

The archaeological evidence, although fragmented, clearly shows a gradual but persistent increase in the presence of cats within human settlements across various regions of Egypt during the late Neolithic and Predynastic periods. This process was not instantaneous but rather evolved over many centuries, likely reflecting a gradual shift in the human perception of felines – from potential competitors for resources to valuable partners in controlling vermin and, ultimately, to sacred beings embodying divine power and protection. Each new archaeological discovery contributes to a richer understanding of the timeline and dynamics of this pivotal relationship. The careful analysis of these clues, coupled with ongoing advancements in archaeological techniques, continues to unveil new facets of the ancient Egyptian human-feline connection, offering glimpses into a past that is both captivating and profoundly revealing about the intricacies of human-animal relationships.

The study of early human-feline interactions in ancient Egypt is an ongoing quest. New archaeological sites are continuously being discovered, and innovative research methods constantly refine our understanding of the past. The story of the domestication of the sacred feline is not a tale with a single, definitive beginning, but rather a complex narrative that unfolds over time, accumulating details and nuances with each new discovery. The current evidence provides a compelling framework for understanding the early stages of this unique interspecies relationship, but future research is sure to further enrich and refine our understanding of this fascinating chapter in human and feline history. As scholars continue to delve deeper into the past, the whispers of Bastet and her feline predecessors become clearer, revealing a story of mutual benefit and evolving reverence that continues to captivate and inspire. The journey from simple co-existence to profound veneration is a testament to the complex and enduring bond between humans and cats, a connection that has left an indelible mark on history and continues to resonate to this day.

Cats in Predynastic Egypt

The Predynastic period in Egypt, spanning roughly from 4000 to 3100 BCE, marks a crucial stage in understanding the evolving relationship between humans and cats. While the definitive evidence of fully domesticated cats remains elusive for this era, the available archaeological and artistic data suggest a burgeoning significance of felines within Predynastic society, laying the groundwork for their later deification. This period reveals the seeds of a relationship that would blossom into full-blown reverence in subsequent dynasties.

One of the primary sources of information is the analysis of Predynastic art. While the artistic styles of this era are markedly different from the highly refined aesthetics of later periods, they offer invaluable glimpses into the worldview of the time. The depictions of cats, though often stylized and less realistic than later representations, are nonetheless significant. Unlike many other animals depicted primarily in hunting or agricultural contexts, cats hold a somewhat unique position. They are not solely represented as prey or sources of food, though such portrayals do exist. Instead, there's a subtle hint of something more, a hint of an evolving symbolic or even spiritual association.

The Naqada II period (circa 3500-3200 BCE), towards the end of the Predynastic era, witnesses a particularly notable increase in the depiction of felines in art. Pottery fragments from this period frequently feature feline motifs, sometimes integrated into more complex scenes depicting daily life or ritualistic activities. For instance, the Gerzean culture, dominant in Upper Egypt during this phase, produced pottery adorned with feline imagery alongside representations of other animals and human figures. The context of these depictions, however, remains a subject of ongoing scholarly debate. Were these representations merely decorative, reflecting the prevalence of cats in the environment? Or did they carry a deeper symbolic meaning, pointing towards an emerging appreciation for the feline's unique attributes?

Detailed analysis of the style and placement of feline motifs on this pottery provides important clues. In some cases, the feline figures are prominently displayed, suggesting a deliberate emphasis on their presence within the artwork. In other instances, felines appear alongside other animals often associated with the hunt or agriculture, perhaps signifying their role in maintaining the balance of nature or contributing to human sustenance through rodent control. The integration of feline imagery into broader compositions suggests that cats were not simply viewed as creatures separate from human life but were already intertwined within their daily activities, whether practical or ritualistic. The careful examination of these artistic details continues to yield crucial insights into the nascent appreciation for cats within Predynastic society.

Furthermore, the study of Predynastic cemeteries offers another crucial perspective. While the practice of elaborate cat burials, characteristic of later dynastic periods, is not yet evident in this era, the discovery of feline remains within some Predynastic burial sites holds considerable significance. These finds, though often less formalized than later examples, suggest a growing association between cats and the human world even beyond life. The context of these discoveries, specifically the proximity to human burials and the inclusion of grave goods, requires careful consideration. Were these instances accidental, simply reflecting the presence of cats in settlements and their potential proximity to burial grounds? Or do they point towards an emerging recognition of cats as something more, possessing qualities deserving of inclusion in burial contexts?

The meticulous examination of these burial sites continues to reveal intriguing patterns. In some instances, feline remains are discovered in close proximity to human interments, while in other cases, they are found in separate but nearby locations. This variation in burial practices indicates a nuanced and evolving relationship, rather than a monolithic view of the feline's significance. It points towards a spectrum of potential meanings, ranging from simple co-existence to something approaching a symbolic or perhaps even spiritual association. Moreover, the analysis of the skeletal remains themselves – including age, sex, and dietary

indicators – offers further insights into the life and role of cats within these Predynastic communities.

While the evidence from Predynastic cemeteries is not as abundant or explicit as that from later periods, its careful analysis reveals a gradual shift in human perception towards felines. The mere presence of feline remains in burial sites, even without the elaborate rituals or grave goods associated with later periods, signifies a growing connection, an acknowledgment of the feline's place within the human world, even in death. This evolving awareness provides critical clues in understanding the early stages of the feline's integration into the spiritual and cultural fabric of Egyptian society.

It is crucial to compare the representation of cats in Predynastic art with that of other animals to appreciate their emerging distinctiveness. While depictions of other animals often emphasize their utilitarian roles – such as hunting, agriculture, or providing food – the representations of cats demonstrate a subtle shift toward symbolic or spiritual significance. The detailed study of the stylistic choices, the positioning within compositions, and the context of their appearance in comparison to other animals within the same artistic pieces, contribute to a more nuanced understanding of the rising status of felines.

The scarcity of unambiguous textual evidence from the Predynastic period limits our understanding, but the archaeological and artistic evidence speak volumes. The gradual accumulation of feline remains in burial sites and their increasingly prominent depiction in art are not coincidental. They suggest an ongoing transformation in human-feline interaction, a shift from a purely utilitarian relationship to one infused with growing symbolic and potentially spiritual significance. This subtle shift laid the foundation for the profound reverence cats would receive in later periods, marking a crucial stage in the long and complex history of the human-feline bond in ancient Egypt.

The ongoing research into Predynastic sites and artifacts continuously refines our understanding of this crucial phase. New discoveries and advancements in analytical techniques, such as isotopic analysis of bone samples or improved dating methods, constantly add to our knowledge. The subtle clues embedded within the artistic representations and burial practices of this era provide invaluable insights into the developing relationship between humans and cats, revealing the early stirrings of a bond that would define the spiritual and cultural landscape of ancient Egypt for millennia to come. The quest to fully understand this pivotal period continues, but the fragments we possess thus far paint a compelling picture of a burgeoning reverence for the feline, a foundation upon which the later deep veneration of cats would be built. The story of cats in Predynastic Egypt is a testament to the enduring power of interspecies relationships and the evolution of beliefs and cultural practices over time. Each new piece of evidence brings us closer to understanding the profound connection between humans and cats that would shape the history of ancient Egypt and continue to fascinate us today.

The Mythological Origins of Bastet

The transition from a practical, utilitarian relationship with cats to the profound religious veneration seen in later periods of ancient Egypt is nowhere more evident than in the evolution of the goddess Bastet. While pinpointing the precise origins of Bastet's worship is challenging due to the scarcity of direct evidence from the earliest periods, piecing together the fragments of art, mythology, and archaeological findings allows us to construct a compelling narrative of her emergence. Unlike the relatively straightforward documentation of later dynasties, tracing Bastet's origins requires a more nuanced approach, combining meticulous analysis of available artifacts with informed speculation based on comparative mythology and the broader context of ancient Egyptian religious development.

The earliest potential connections to Bastet's lineage appear in Predynastic art, albeit in a highly ambiguous and symbolic form. The feline motifs present on pottery shards and other artifacts from this period, as discussed previously, lack the definitive features that clearly identify a goddess. Yet, certain artistic conventions and recurring patterns suggest a potential link. The stylized feline figures, often depicted in a seated or watchful posture, might represent a nascent form of feline deity, a precursor to the more fully developed iconography of later periods. It's crucial to remember that these interpretations are tentative, relying heavily on contextual analysis and a degree of scholarly inference. The absence of definitive inscriptions or clear religious contexts makes definitive claims difficult. However, these early representations lay the groundwork for a deeper examination of the transition from simple feline motifs to the fully formed goddess Bastet.

The Old Kingdom (circa 2686-2181 BCE) offers a more concrete, though still fragmented, picture of Bastet's developing role. While she doesn't emerge as the fully realized goddess of Bubastis at this stage, the increasing prominence of feline imagery in religious contexts suggests a growing association between cats and divine power. In this era, the lioness goddess Sekhmet takes center stage, a powerful warrior goddess associated with protection, destruction, and healing. Sekhmet's powerful image, often depicted as a fearsome lioness with a bloodthirsty rage, foreshadows certain aspects of Bastet's later character. However, Bastet's gentler, more domestic nature remains largely undeveloped during the Old Kingdom. This suggests a potential evolutionary path, with Bastet's character perhaps developing as a gentler, more nurturing counterpoint to the fierce Sekhmet. The presence of lioness deities in this early period provides a vital framework for understanding the later development of Bastet's iconography and attributes. The gradual evolution from powerful, fearsome lioness figures to the more domestic, protective cat goddess suggests a complex interplay between ancient Egyptian beliefs regarding the nature of power and protection.

The Middle Kingdom (circa 2055-1650 BCE) witnesses a shift toward a more refined and consistent representation of feline goddesses. While the precise moment of Bastet's emergence as a distinct deity remains unclear, this period shows a significant increase in the number and quality of representations directly associated with her cult. The transition from ambiguous feline motifs to more clearly defined feline goddesses, with specific attributes and roles, marks a significant turning point in understanding the evolution of Bastet's worship. The development of specialized symbols, rituals, and cult centers associated with feline goddesses during this period points towards a growing institutionalization of their worship, which would solidify their position within the Egyptian religious pantheon.

The emergence of Bubastis as a major religious center during the Middle Kingdom strongly suggests the rising prominence of a feline goddess in this region, likely the goddess we now know as Bastet. The growing evidence of sophisticated religious structures, dedicated priests, and elaborate rituals associated with Bubastis lends weight to the theory that Bastet's cult originated or at least significantly developed during the Middle Kingdom. The discovery of artifacts and inscriptions associated with this site provides vital information on the rituals, beliefs, and iconography associated with Bastet's worship, illuminating her increasing importance within the religious landscape of ancient Egypt.

The New Kingdom (circa 1550-1069 BCE) firmly establishes Bastet as a major goddess within the Egyptian pantheon. She is now clearly depicted as a domestic cat, often depicted wearing a sun disk and holding a sistrum, a musical instrument used in religious ceremonies. This distinctive iconography further emphasizes her role as a protector and a benevolent deity. The association with the sun disk highlights a connection to the divine power and royalty, further emphasizing her importance within the religious hierarchy. Her gentler nature, contrasted with the ferocity of Sekhmet, becomes a central aspect of her cult and a source of comfort for the faithful.

The transition from earlier, more ambiguous feline representations to the distinctly identifiable image of Bastet as a domestic cat, wearing a sun disk and holding a sistrum, represents a significant development in her iconography. This specific visual representation likely emerged gradually, developing over centuries from earlier artistic conventions and symbolic meanings. The evolution of Bastet's image reflects the changing religious landscape and the growing sophistication of Egyptian art and religious practice.

Bastet's attributes throughout these periods highlight a fascinating interplay between power and domesticity. While she inherits some aspects of the ferocity associated with earlier lioness goddesses, she's primarily known for her protective and nurturing qualities. She is the guardian of the home, the protector of women, children, and cats themselves. This association with domesticity, combined with her benevolent nature, differentiates her significantly from other feline goddesses, cementing her unique position within the Egyptian pantheon. This gentle aspect of her character likely contributed to the widespread popular appeal of her cult, making her a beloved deity across social classes and geographical regions.

It's important to consider the possibility of influences from other cultures in the development of Bastet's mythology. While the specifics remain debated, the presence of similar feline deities in neighboring regions suggests potential cross-cultural exchange. However, the uniquely Egyptian aspects of Bastet's mythology, iconography, and religious practices highlight the distinctive nature of her worship within the Egyptian cultural context. Comparative studies with other ancient Near Eastern cultures, specifically those with feline goddesses or similar symbolic representations of cats, might shed further light on the potential influences and interactions that contributed to Bastet's unique development. The ongoing research into comparative mythology continues to refine our understanding of the complex cultural exchanges that shaped ancient Egyptian religious beliefs.

The evolution of Bastet's iconography, attributes, and mythological associations mirrors the changing religious landscape of ancient Egypt. The transition from earlier, ambiguous feline depictions to the clear and distinctive image of the domestic cat goddess reveals a complex interplay between ancient beliefs, artistic conventions, and cultural exchange. Her character, a blend of power and domesticity, speaks volumes about the multifaceted view of felines within ancient Egyptian society and its evolving understanding of the sacred. The story of Bastet's rise to prominence, therefore, isn't just a religious narrative; it is a reflection of the profound and enduring connection between humanity and cats within ancient Egypt. The ongoing research into Bastet's origins continues to illuminate this fascinating chapter in the history of religious beliefs and the human-animal bond. Each new discovery brings us closer to a richer and more nuanced understanding of the goddess and her enduring legacy.

Religious Significance of Cats in Early Dynastic Egypt

The Early Dynastic Period (circa 3100-2686 BCE) marks a pivotal era in the history of ancient Egypt, a time of unification and the establishment of a centralized state. While the full extent of cat worship is more vividly portrayed in later periods, the seeds of this profound reverence were sown during this formative time. The available evidence, though fragmented, hints at an evolving relationship between humans and cats, moving beyond simple utility towards a recognition of their spiritual significance. The absence of extensive written records from this period necessitates a multi-faceted approach, relying heavily on archaeological evidence—tomb paintings, artifacts, and skeletal remains—to piece together the religious context of the time.

One of the primary sources of information for understanding the role of cats in Early Dynastic religion comes from tomb paintings. While not as elaborate or numerous as those from later periods, the existing murals offer glimpses into the daily life and beliefs of the elite. Several tombs depict cats alongside other domestic animals, suggesting their integration into the household and, possibly, the broader community. However, the significance of these depictions goes beyond mere representation of domestic life. The careful positioning of the cats within the artistic compositions, often near other symbolic elements associated with fertility or the afterlife, hints at a developing sense of their sacredness. These artistic choices, although subtle, suggest a growing recognition of cats as more than simply utilitarian animals. Further research is needed to decipher the exact meaning conveyed in the context of specific motifs and the positioning of feline images within each artistic narrative. For example, the inclusion of a cat near offerings or images of deceased family members could imply a protective role or a connection to the afterlife, a theme which becomes central in later Egyptian religious beliefs.

The limited number of intact tombs from the Early Dynastic Period significantly restricts the information available to scholars. Many sites have been disturbed over millennia, leaving us with fragmented evidence that necessitates careful interpretation and cross-referencing. However, some recently excavated tombs have yielded invaluable artifacts that cast more light on the status of cats. These artifacts, including small figurines and amulets depicting cats in various poses, suggest the creation of early cat-related cult objects. The meticulous craftsmanship of these artifacts, often found associated with the deceased, indicates the considerable importance placed upon cats even in these early stages of Egyptian history. The existence of such ritualistic artifacts signifies the development of early cat-related religious practices, even if the full rituals and beliefs remain shrouded in mystery. The discovery of such artifact's fuels further research into workshops and the societal structure related to the production of these early cat-related artifacts. The complexity and detail embedded within many of the small figurines suggest dedicated artisans, pointing to a possible established structure related to these early cat cults.

The skeletal remains of cats unearthed in Early Dynastic Period tombs and settlements offer another valuable, if sometimes less direct, line of evidence. The careful burial of cats, sometimes with elaborate grave goods, indicates a deliberate practice that goes beyond the simple disposal of animals. The presence of cat bones in tombs raises important questions regarding their role in funerary rituals. Were they seen as companions to the deceased, or did they hold a more symbolic significance? Were cats sacrificed or did they die naturally and then receive a special burial? These questions, while complex, highlight the importance of analyzing the context of these remains within the larger archaeological framework. The presence of grave goods associated with certain feline burials suggests that these cats held special status during their lives, deserving specific rituals following their death. This practice suggests that the status of some cats was elevated well above that of a simple domestic pet.

It is important to note the distinction between "domestication" and "domesticity." While cats were certainly integrated into the lives of ancient Egyptians during the Early Dynastic Period, the evidence for complete domestication is complex. Evidence suggests that cats played a significant role in controlling vermin, essential in the early agrarian society, but it was the

development of strong religious beliefs that profoundly shaped their status. The transition from utilitarian relationship to that of reverence marks a crucial shift in the perception of these felines. The early integration of cats into the fabric of daily life is an essential step towards their eventual elevation to god-like status, which is fully apparent in later periods. This gradual shift requires further research to determine the precise timeline and interplay between practical needs and emerging spiritual significance.

The analysis of available textual evidence from the Early Dynastic Period is limited, due to the scarcity of extant writings. The hieroglyphic script was still in its developmental stages, and much of what was written was likely associated with administrative tasks rather than elaborate theological treatises. However, the limited inscriptions we do have—those found on artifacts or in the few surviving tomb texts—provide valuable clues. Researchers carefully analyze these inscriptions for any mentions of cats, and the context in which such mentions appear. Even seemingly insignificant references can contribute significantly to our understanding of the cat's evolving role in religious and societal structures. The absence of extensive written documentation from this time necessitates a greater emphasis on archaeological analysis and cross-referencing between various forms of evidence. Every fragment of text, every small artifact, every skeletal find contributes to a crucial piece of the puzzle.

The Early Dynastic Period laid the groundwork for the sophisticated cat cults that flourished in later Egyptian history. While the evidence is more fragmented and less overtly religious than that of later dynasties, it nonetheless indicates the rising status of cats within ancient Egyptian society. The subtle presence of cats in tomb paintings, the creation of specialized cat-related artifacts, and the careful burial practices surrounding feline remains all point towards a slowly growing reverence for these animals. This reverence laid the groundwork for the widespread and intense cat worship seen in later periods. The subtle clues from the Early Dynastic Period provide essential context for understanding the full scale of the religious significance of cats in ancient Egypt, offering a foundation for future research and discoveries that will further clarify this fascinating and often-misunderstood chapter of ancient Egyptian history. The gradual evolution of feline representation and religious significance, from practical companions to revered deities, underscores the importance of this transitional period. The future discovery of new sites and careful reassessment of existing evidence will inevitably further refine our understanding of this crucial era in the history of the sacred feline in ancient Egypt. The interplay between practical considerations and evolving spiritual beliefs will continue to be a subject of much research.

The Economic Role of Cats in Ancient Egypt

The reverence afforded to cats in ancient Egypt extended far beyond mere religious symbolism; they played a vital, albeit often overlooked, economic role in the daily lives of the Egyptians. Their prowess in controlling vermin, specifically rodents, had a profound impact on the agricultural economy, the foundation of ancient Egyptian society. The Nile Valley, while fertile, was also a breeding ground for rodents that posed a significant threat to stored grain and other essential food supplies. The presence of cats, therefore, was not simply a matter of preference or religious devotion; it was a matter of economic survival.

The importance of grain storage in ancient Egypt cannot be overstated. The annual flooding of the Nile, while essential for agriculture, also presented a challenge. The abundance of grain harvested during the inundation had to be carefully stored to provide sustenance throughout the year. Granaries, often large and elaborately constructed, served as the lifeblood of the Egyptian economy. These structures, however, were vulnerable to infestations of rodents, which could quickly decimate stored grain reserves, leading to famine and economic instability. The protection of these granaries, therefore, was a matter of paramount importance.

While various methods were employed to safeguard grain stores, the role of cats as natural pest control agents was undoubtedly crucial. Cats, with their innate hunting instincts and agility, were perfectly suited to this task. Their presence in granaries and homes would have significantly reduced rodent populations, minimizing the damage to stored food and preventing substantial economic losses. The economic value of this natural pest control should not be underestimated, particularly considering the lack of sophisticated pest management techniques in ancient times. The cost-effectiveness of utilizing cats compared to other potential methods, such as manual rodent control or the construction of elaborate, rodent-proof storage facilities, makes the economic contribution of cats even more remarkable.

Ancient Egyptian texts, though not explicitly focused on the economic contributions of cats, offer occasional glimpses into their practical use. While the focus of many texts lies on the religious and symbolic aspects of cats, some administrative documents, such as those related to the management of royal estates or temple resources, may inadvertently reveal details about their practical employment. For instance, inventories of temple possessions or records of agricultural yields might indirectly indicate the presence and implicit value of cats in safeguarding stored food supplies. Furthermore, the meticulous record-keeping characteristic of ancient Egyptian bureaucracy might reveal patterns or correlations that indirectly support the significance of feline pest control in maintaining economic stability. Deciphering such clues requires careful examination of diverse textual sources, looking beyond explicit mentions of cats to understand their implied role in maintaining the economic vitality of ancient Egypt.

The artistic representations in tomb paintings and other artistic media further support the practical significance of cats. While many depictions focus on the religious and symbolic aspects of cats, some murals or relief carvings subtly depict cats within domestic settings, often near granaries or other storage areas. These seemingly insignificant details, when analyzed collectively, reveal a broader picture of the practical roles cats fulfilled in ancient Egyptian society. The inclusion of cats in such contexts, though not always explicitly stated, implies their role in protecting food supplies and contributing to the overall economic stability of households and communities. The frequency with which cats appear in such depictions, in contrast to other domestic animals, indicates their relatively high value and significant contribution to the daily economy.

The architectural design of ancient Egyptian homes and granaries may also have been influenced by the need to integrate cats into pest control strategies. While there is no direct evidence to support this claim, it is plausible that features of homes and granaries may have been designed to accommodate the presence of cats, enhancing their effectiveness in rodent control. The design of granaries, for instance, might have included specific access points or

features that facilitated feline movement and access to potential rodent habitats. Similarly, domestic architecture might have incorporated features that provided shelter and comfortable spaces for cats to reside, further promoting their integration into the household ecosystem. While this remains, a topic requiring further research, considering the interplay between architectural design and feline pest control could provide valuable insights into the economic role of cats in ancient Egypt.

Beyond their role in protecting grain stores, cats also provided crucial pest control services in homes and other areas where stored food and other valuables were kept. Rodents posed a constant threat to domestic supplies, textiles, and other goods. The presence of cats within homes would have significantly reduced the risk of damage and loss, providing an essential service that contributed to the overall economic well-being of households. The value of this service is often underestimated when considering the economic impact of cats, but its contribution to reducing losses of domestic goods should not be overlooked. The importance of this role underscores the multifaceted nature of the economic contributions of cats in ancient Egypt.

Furthermore, the economic impact of cats extended beyond direct pest control. Their value as hunting companions, particularly in hunting smaller animals like birds and reptiles, may have also contributed to the overall food supply. While less significant compared to their role in rodent control, this aspect of their economic contribution underscores the multifaceted value of cats in the ancient Egyptian context. This added benefit, although less significant than their primary role in pest control, further highlights the varied ways in which cats contributed to the economy.

The economic significance of cats in ancient Egypt is therefore a complex issue that requires careful consideration of various lines of evidence. While many studies focus on the religious and symbolic aspects of cat veneration, the practical economic contributions of these animals should not be dismissed as insignificant. Their role in controlling vermin, protecting food supplies, and contributing to the overall economic stability of households and communities makes their impact on ancient Egyptian society undeniable. Further research into this aspect of cat-human interaction in ancient Egypt is needed, examining various textual, artistic, and archaeological evidence to provide a more comprehensive understanding of the economic role of the revered feline. This deeper understanding will provide a more complete picture of the complex and multifaceted relationship between ancient Egyptians and their feline companions, transcending the often-emphasized religious and symbolic aspects to reveal the significant practical and economic dimensions of this relationship. The interwoven threads of practicality and piety, utility and veneration, form a rich tapestry that showcases the profound and enduring significance of cats in the daily life and economy of ancient Egypt.

Bastet's Iconography and Attributes

Chapter Two

Bastet's multifaceted nature is perhaps best understood through the evolution of her iconography. Her visual representation, far from static, underwent significant transformations throughout the millennia, reflecting shifting religious beliefs, cultural trends, and the evolving relationship between humans and felines in ancient Egypt. While the most widely recognized image of Bastet is that of a domestic cat, a gentle, almost playful creature, her earliest depictions reveal a more formidable and powerful aspect.

In the Predynastic Period and early Dynastic Era, Bastet was frequently depicted as a lioness, a fierce and protective predator. This portrayal emphasized her connection to Sekhmet, the fearsome lion-headed goddess of war and disease. The lioness, a symbol of strength, courage, and royal power, was a fitting representation for a goddess associated with protection and retribution. Statuettes and reliefs from this period frequently show Bastet as a powerful lioness, often bearing the sun disk and uraeus, symbols of royal authority and divine power. These early depictions underscore Bastet's role as a defender, a warrior goddess capable of unleashing the fury of the desert sun against her enemies. The aggressive posture, often with bared teeth and a determined gaze, highlights her ferocity and capacity for fierce protection. These early images are starkly different from the more familiar, domesticated cat image associated with her later representation. The transition from lioness to house cat reflects a significant shift in the understanding of her character and her relationship with the people.

The shift from a lioness to a domestic cat as Bastet's primary form is not a sudden transformation but a gradual evolution, reflecting changing religious and cultural perspectives. The lioness continued to be present in Bastet's iconography but gradually decreased in frequency as the domestic cat form gained prominence. The reasons for this change are complex and likely intertwined with various social and religious factors. The growing domestication of cats in ancient Egypt likely played a significant role in this transformation. As cats became more integrated into daily life, their role in protecting homes and granaries from pests became more apparent. This close association between cats and domestic life likely influenced the perception of Bastet, leading to a more gentle and approachable representation.

The transformation also reflected the growing importance of lower Egypt, the region where Bastet's cult was centered. Lower Egypt was known for its rich agricultural lands and its focus on domestic life, in contrast to Upper Egypt's more militaristic character. The domestic cat, a symbol of domesticity and fertility, became a more appropriate representation of Bastet as her cult became more associated with the peaceful and prosperous life of the

Nile Delta. This association with domesticity is underscored in numerous artistic depictions, often showing Bastet in a relaxed posture, playing with kittens, or in the company of other household animals. This gentler side of Bastet, a nurturing and protective mother figure, contrasts starkly with the fierce lioness of earlier representations.

The domestic cat form of Bastet became particularly prominent during the New Kingdom and later periods. Statuettes, amulets, and other artistic representations frequently depict her as a sleek, graceful cat, often adorned with jewelry or seated on a throne. The cat's ears are typically erect, its expression calm and serene, a far cry from the aggressive stance of the earlier lioness representations. The shift also reflects a changing emphasis within her cult. Instead of focusing on her warrior aspects, the emphasis shifted towards her roles as a protector of homes, families, and women in childbirth.

This shift in iconography is mirrored in the attributes associated with Bastet. While earlier depictions frequently emphasized weapons and symbols of warfare, later representations focus more on symbols of fertility, motherhood, and domestic bliss. The sistrum, a musical instrument often depicted in Bastet's hands, became a significant symbol of her role in music, dance, and celebration. This association with joyous festivities is a significant departure from her earlier, more militant character. The sistrum's rhythmic sound was believed to ward off evil and bring good fortune. This subtle shift in Bastet's attributes is a telling reflection of the evolving nature of her cult and her relationship with the people she protected.

The presence of kittens frequently accompanying Bastet further emphasizes this aspect of motherhood and fertility. These depictions not only highlight her nurturing side but also reflect the ancient Egyptian belief in the regenerative power of cats. Their ability to give birth to large litters symbolized abundance and prosperity. The association of Bastet with childbirth and the safe delivery of infants reinforced her role as a protector of women and children. The presence of the menat necklace, often seen in depictions of Isis and other goddesses associated with motherhood, further reinforces this association.

Further examination of Bastet's iconography reveals subtle variations in her depiction depending on the specific context. For instance, Bastet's representation in funerary contexts often emphasized her role as a guide to the afterlife. In these depictions, she is sometimes shown with an ankh, the symbol of life, or with other symbols associated with the underworld. The context within which Bastet was depicted significantly altered her interpretation and symbolic meaning. This nuanced approach to Bastet's iconography underscores the adaptable and versatile nature of her religious role in ancient Egypt.

The materials used in creating Bastet's images also provide significant insights into her evolving character. Early representations were frequently carved from wood or stone, reflecting her powerful and almost untouchable nature. However, during the later periods, smaller, more intimate statuettes were made from less expensive materials, such as faience or bronze. These more accessible representations suggest a closer, more personal connection between worshippers and the goddess, reflecting a shift towards a more intimate and less awe-inspiring form of devotion.

The variety of forms in which Bastet was portrayed—as a lioness, a cat, a woman with a cat's head—reflects the complex nature of her role in the pantheon and her adaptability to changing religious and social dynamics. Each representation, from the fierce lioness to the gentle domestic cat, highlighted a specific facet of her character, reflecting the ancient Egyptian belief in the multifaceted nature of divinity. This multifaceted nature allowed Bastet to resonate with different aspects of Egyptian life and beliefs, ensuring her continued veneration throughout the different periods of ancient Egyptian history.

The study of Bastet's iconography is not simply an exercise in art history; it is a window into the evolving religious beliefs, social structures, and cultural values of ancient Egypt. By carefully examining the changes in her visual representation and associated attributes, we gain a deeper understanding of the profound and enduring relationship between humans and cats in ancient Egypt and the complex nature of Bastet herself. Her visual legacy provides invaluable insights into the fascinating world of ancient Egyptian religion and mythology, weaving together historical fact and symbolic meaning in a compelling narrative. The enduring appeal of Bastet lies in her adaptability and capacity to represent various facets of the human experience, from protection and power to motherhood and domesticity. Her image, evolving over centuries, continues to inspire awe and fascination, demonstrating the enduring connection between ancient Egyptians and their feline goddess. The enduring legacy of Bastet serves as a potent reminder of the enduring relationship between humans and animals, a relationship that transcends time and culture.

Bastet's Temples and Cult Centers

The geographical distribution of Bastet's worship offers valuable insights into the evolution and reach of her cult. While her influence extended throughout Egypt, certain locations served as principal centers, attracting pilgrims and housing significant temples dedicated to her veneration. The most prominent of these, undoubtedly, was Bubastis, a city whose very name is intrinsically linked to the goddess. Located in the northeastern Nile Delta, Bubastis held a position of paramount importance within Bastet's cult, evolving from a relatively modest settlement to a thriving metropolis, largely due to its religious significance.

The temple of Bastet at Bubastis was a monumental structure, its construction spanning centuries and reflecting the ever-growing devotion to the feline goddess. Archaeological evidence suggests a series of expansions and renovations, each reflecting the changing political and economic fortunes of the city and the overarching religious landscape of ancient Egypt. While much of the temple lies in ruins today, remnants of its grandeur remain, testament to its once-imposing presence. The temple's layout likely followed a standard Egyptian pattern, encompassing various courts, pylons, and hypostyle halls, each dedicated to specific rituals and aspects of Bastet's worship. The massive pylons, decorated with intricate reliefs and inscriptions, served as symbolic gateways to the sacred precinct, their towering presence announcing the importance of the site. These pylons were not merely architectural elements; they were imbued with symbolic meaning, signifying the threshold between the mundane world and the sacred realm of the goddess.

The hypostyle halls, with their rows of massive columns supporting the roof, created an awe-inspiring atmosphere, conducive to religious awe and reverence. These halls were likely the sites of major religious ceremonies, processions, and festivals in honor of Bastet. The sheer scale of the structure would have been overwhelming to the pilgrims, emphasizing the power and majesty of the goddess. The walls of these halls, like the pylons, were richly decorated, featuring scenes depicting the goddess in her various manifestations, along with narratives illustrating her myths and legends. These visual narratives served as a powerful form of religious instruction, reinforcing the beliefs and practices associated with Bastet's worship.

Beyond the main temple complex, the city of Bubastis likely contained numerous smaller shrines and chapels dedicated to Bastet, catering to the diverse religious needs of the city's inhabitants. These smaller structures might have been located within private homes, public spaces, or associated with specific guilds or professions. Their existence underscores the pervasive nature of Bastet's worship within Bubastis, permeating all aspects of daily life.

The annual festival of Bastet at Bubastis was a truly remarkable event, drawing massive crowds from across Egypt. This pilgrimage, described by ancient Greek historians, was a spectacle of religious fervor and celebration, involving elaborate processions, musical performances, and ecstatic rituals. The sheer scale of the festival and the number of participants underscore the centrality of Bastet's cult in ancient Egyptian society. The festival's significance extended beyond mere religious observance; it was a crucial social event, bringing people together from diverse social backgrounds and reinforcing community bonds.

However, Bubastis was not the sole center of Bastet's worship. Other locations throughout Egypt housed temples and shrines dedicated to her, albeit on a smaller scale. These sites, scattered across the country, reflect the widespread reverence for Bastet and the varied aspects of her multifaceted character. For instance, in Lower Egypt, numerous smaller temples and shrines dedicated to Bastet were found in close proximity to the Nile River and in major agricultural centers. This spatial distribution highlights her association with fertility, prosperity, and domestic protection, reflecting the critical role she played in the lives of ordinary Egyptians.

In Upper Egypt, the presence of Bastet's cult was less pronounced, suggesting a regional difference in the goddess's prominence. While she might not have enjoyed the same level of prominence as in Lower Egypt, her presence in Upper Egyptian temples and shrines highlights the goddess's overarching importance across the entire nation. This presence, albeit more limited, suggests that Bastet's protective aspects resonated with the people of Upper Egypt as well, even if her association with domesticity and fertility might have been less emphasized.

The architectural style and design of Bastet's temples varied depending on their location and the period of construction. However, several common features suggest a consistent thematic approach to her representation. The use of specific colors, such as gold and blue, may have reflected the celestial and divine aspects of Bastet. The inclusion of certain symbolic elements, such as the sistrum and the menat necklace, emphasized her roles as a protector and a goddess associated with fertility and motherhood. The choice of materials, ranging from durable stone to more fragile materials like faience, also reflects the varying levels of devotion and the economic capacity of those constructing the shrines.

The organization of temple complexes at these different sites, including the layout of courts, the positioning of sanctuaries, and the orientation of buildings, suggests a clear understanding of spatial symbolism. The placement of certain structures in relation to others reinforced the hierarchical relationships within the pantheon and the specific aspects of Bastet's divine character emphasized at each location. The architectural and spatial organization of these complexes provided a tangible expression of the religious beliefs and practices associated with Bastet's cult.

Beyond the architectural features, the rituals and practices performed at Bastet's temples and cult centers offer further insights into her worship. The annual festivals, already mentioned in the context of Bubastis, were not unique to that city. Smaller-scale festivals and ceremonies were likely held at other Bastet temples and shrines throughout the year, providing opportunities for the local population to express their devotion. These festivals may have involved processions, offerings of food and drink, musical performances, and ritual dances.

The offerings made to Bastet varied depending on the context and the specific aspects of the goddess being invoked. Food, drink, and incense were common offerings, reflecting the ancient Egyptian practice of appeasing deities through material gifts. However, other offerings, such as jewelry, amulets, and figurines, suggest that devotees also sought to express their devotion through more personal and valuable items. These offerings were not merely acts of piety; they were also symbolic representations of the worshipper's relationship with the goddess.

The presence of specific symbols and iconographic elements within the temples and shrines also offers insights into the religious practices and beliefs associated with Bastet's cult. The sistrum, for instance, was a prominent symbol within many Bastet temples, its rhythmic sound believed to have played an important role in ritualistic activities. The presence of other symbols, such as the ankh, the uraeus, and various feline representations, further emphasized the goddess' associations with life, royalty, and protection.

In conclusion, the study of Bastet's temples and cult centers provides a multifaceted perspective on her worship and her role within ancient Egyptian society. These sites were not merely architectural structures; they were dynamic centers of religious activity, social interaction, and cultural expression. Their analysis allows us to unravel the complex tapestry of religious beliefs, ritual practices, and social structures associated with Bastet's cult, shedding light on the enduring legacy of this feline goddess. The distribution of her temples across Egypt, their architectural design, and the ritual practices performed within them reflect the multifaceted nature of Bastet herself and the profound relationship between ancient Egyptians and their feline deity. The ongoing archaeological research and analysis of these sites continue to unveil new insights into the fascinating world of ancient Egyptian religion and mythology.

Bastet's Roles in Egyptian Mythology

Bastet's multifaceted nature is perhaps best understood by examining her diverse roles within the complex tapestry of Egyptian mythology. While primarily known as the goddess of cats, protection, and domesticity, her influence extended far beyond these immediate associations. Her involvement in numerous myths and legends reveals a deity with a surprisingly complex and nuanced character, reflecting the intricate beliefs and practices of ancient Egyptian society.

One of Bastet's most prominent roles was that of a protector. She was invoked for protection against evil spirits, disease, and other harmful forces. Her association with cats, believed to possess an innate ability to ward off malevolent entities, reinforced this protective aspect. Amulets and figurines depicting Bastet were frequently used as talismans, providing their owners with a sense of security and divine protection. These amulets, often intricately crafted from precious materials like gold and faience, were worn as personal ornaments, embedded in jewelry, or even placed within tombs as a form of protection for the deceased in their journey to the afterlife. The widespread use of these protective items demonstrates the depth of Bastet's protective role in the daily lives of ancient Egyptians, encompassing both the living and the dead.

Beyond individual protection, Bastet was also considered a protector of the home and family. She was invoked to ensure the safety and prosperity of households, safeguarding their inhabitants from harm and misfortune. This role as a domestic goddess further solidified her connection to the everyday lives of ordinary Egyptians. Her image often adorned household shrines, emphasizing her close proximity to family life and her ability to offer comfort and security within the domestic sphere. The reverence shown to Bastet within the home reflects the integral role that the goddess played in maintaining the stability and harmony of ancient Egyptian families. The domestic sphere, far from being a purely secular space, was often imbued with religious significance, with deities like Bastet playing a crucial role in maintaining order and well-being.

Bastet's association with fertility is another crucial aspect of her mythology. Her connection to cats, known for their prolific reproductive abilities, contributed to this association. Furthermore, Bastet was often depicted holding a sistrum, a musical instrument that was believed to have fertility-enhancing properties. The rhythmic shaking of the sistrum during religious ceremonies might have been symbolically linked to the act of creation and the renewal of life. This connection to fertility expanded beyond individual reproduction; it extended to the bounty of the land and the overall prosperity of the community. The goddess was thus viewed as a guarantor of a successful harvest and the general well-being of the agricultural community, which was the backbone of ancient Egyptian society. Her role in fertility connected her deeply to the cyclical rhythms of nature and the life-giving power of the Nile River, the very source of Egypt's prosperity and abundance.

The feline goddess wasn't merely a protector and a fertility symbol. Ancient texts and artwork depict her as a passionate dancer and musician, linked to the joys of life and celebrations. Her association with music and dance further humanizes the goddess, revealing a more vibrant and engaging aspect of her character. The sistrum, in addition to its fertility-related connotations, was also a musical instrument, central to religious ceremonies and festive occasions dedicated to Bastet. The rhythmic sounds produced by the sistrum, played by priestesses during rituals, might have induced a state of ecstasy and spiritual communion, bringing worshippers closer to the divine realm. The goddess's association with music and dance thus added a layer of celebratory fervor to her worship, transforming religious observances into engaging and uplifting experiences. The festivals held in her honor, as described by ancient Greek historians like Herodotus, were vivid spectacles of music, dance, and collective celebration, underlining Bastet's joyous and exuberant nature.

Bastet's relationships with other deities add further complexity to her narrative. Her connections to Sekhmet, the fierce lion-headed goddess of war and disease, and Hathor, the goddess of love, beauty, and motherhood, are particularly noteworthy. While often seen as distinct entities, Sekhmet and Bastet shared aspects of their divine powers; representing different facets of the feminine divine. Sekhmet's fierce wrath, associated with protection and retribution, contrasted with Bastet's gentler, more protective nature, but both were capable of immense power and were revered for their capacity to defend the righteous. Similarly, Bastet's association with motherhood and nurturing mirrors attributes associated with Hathor. These connections highlight the fluidity and interconnectedness within the Egyptian pantheon, indicating that deities were not always neatly compartmentalized but rather possessed overlapping attributes and shared domains of influence. The interplay between Bastet's roles highlights the rich and dynamic nature of the ancient Egyptian religious system, where gods and goddesses interacted, and their attributes sometimes blurred the lines between distinct deities.

Mythological narratives further illuminate Bastet's role and character. While fewer myths explicitly center on Bastet compared to some other major deities, her presence in various stories adds to our understanding of her attributes and her interactions with other gods and mortals. For example, her connection with Sekhmet in some narratives indicates a complex interplay between destructive power and nurturing protection. In these narratives, Bastet often acts as a mediating force, helping to control or channel Sekhmet's destructive energies. Similarly, stories involving Bastet's interactions with humans illustrate her role as a protector and benefactor, highlighting her involvement in both the daily lives of ordinary people and in broader cosmic events. This interplay between her protector role and her involvement in significant events further enhances her importance in the Egyptian pantheon and emphasizes her capacity to intervene in both mundane and extraordinary matters.

The study of Bastet's roles in Egyptian mythology reveals a goddess whose influence extended far beyond the simple association with cats. Her protective nature, her link to fertility, her association with music and dance, and her relationships with other deities paint a portrait of a multifaceted and dynamic figure, deeply embedded in the cultural and religious life of ancient Egypt. Her image, found throughout Egypt in temples, amulets, and artwork, serves as a testament to the enduring influence of this beloved feline goddess and her profound connection to the beliefs and practices of ancient Egyptian society.

Further research into surviving texts and archaeological findings continues to reveal new facets of Bastet's multifaceted character, reinforcing her position as one of the most enduring and captivating deities in the ancient Egyptian pantheon. The ongoing scholarly effort to unearth and interpret these historical fragments allows for a progressively richer understanding of the complex world of ancient Egyptian religion and mythology. The continued exploration of these sources helps shed light not only on Bastet but also on the broader cultural and religious context of ancient Egypt, offering a glimpse into the rich tapestry of beliefs that shaped this remarkable civilization.

Festivals and Rituals Honoring Bastet

The worship of Bastet, the cat goddess, wasn't confined to private devotions and the offering of small gifts at home shrines. Her veneration manifested most vibrantly during the numerous festivals held annually in her honor. These weren't merely religious occasions; they were crucial social events that structured the rhythm of life in ancient Egyptian communities, especially in Bubastis, her principal cult center. The scale and significance of these festivals offer invaluable insights into the social fabric of ancient Egypt, illuminating the interplay between religious beliefs, social structures, and daily life.

Accounts from Greek historians like Herodotus, albeit filtered through a foreign lens, provide glimpses into the spectacular nature of Bastet's festivals. He describes the annual festival at Bubastis as a massive gathering, drawing pilgrims from across Egypt and even beyond its borders. The sheer volume of participants, estimated in the hundreds of thousands, speaks volumes about the goddess's widespread popularity and the unifying power of her worship. These processions, often traveling by boat along the

Nile, were not just religious pilgrimages; they were also opportunities for social interaction, trade, and celebration. The river, itself a vital life source, became a conduit for both spiritual and social convergence. The journey to Bubastis was, in itself, a significant part of the festival experience, fostering community bonds and solidifying the collective identity of Bastet's followers.

Herodotus's descriptions paint vivid pictures of the celebratory atmosphere: music, dancing, feasting, and general merriment characterized the festival's ambiance. This wasn't the somber, austere religious observance of some other cultures. Instead, Bastet's festivals were joyous occasions, reflecting her association with pleasure, music, and the lighter aspects of life. The abundance of food and drink, the vibrant rhythms of music and dance, and the sheer scale of the gathering created an atmosphere of shared ecstasy, reinforcing the communal bonds among participants. The festive atmosphere is further evidence of Bastet's dual nature – both protector and bringer of joy, weaving her role into the very fabric of daily life.

The rituals themselves were diverse and reflected the multifaceted nature of Bastet's powers. While specific details often remain elusive due to the fragmentary nature of the surviving evidence, the overarching themes of protection, fertility, and celebration are clearly evident. The processions, often involving elaborate floats carrying statues of Bastet and other deities, represented a symbolic journey to the divine. The rhythmic chants and music, created by the sistrum and other instruments, are believed to have induced a state of altered consciousness, allowing for a closer connection with the goddess. The use of music and ritualistic movement acted as conduits to the divine, transforming the physical act of participation into a spiritual experience.

Sacrifices formed a significant component of Bastet's festivals. While cats held a special place in her worship, evidence suggests that other animals, as well as food offerings, were also presented to the goddess. The nature and scale of these sacrifices varied depending on the specific festival and the community involved. However, the act of sacrifice was not simply a matter of appeasement; it was a ritualistic act of communion, symbolically linking the community to the divine realm. The offerings were not merely presented; they were presented with specific rituals, creating a sacred space where the physical and spiritual realms intersected. The careful preparation and execution of these rituals reflected the depth of devotion and the profound significance of the religious act itself.

The archaeological record offers further insights into these festivals. Excavations at Bubastis and other sites have unearthed numerous artifacts associated with Bastet's worship, providing tangible evidence of her widespread veneration. These artifacts, including figurines, amulets, votive offerings, and even the remains of animal sacrifices, paint a detailed picture of the rituals and the intense religious fervor of the time. The sheer quantity of these objects, many of them intricately crafted, speaks to the profound importance of Bastet in the lives of ancient

Egyptians. The artifacts found are not simply religious items; they also tell stories about the artistry, craftsmanship, and social organization of the time.

The impact of Bastet's festivals extended far beyond the immediate participants. These events played a crucial role in the economic and social life of ancient Egypt. The influx of pilgrims to Bubastis generated substantial economic activity, boosting local trade and stimulating the broader Egyptian economy. The festivals provided opportunities for merchants to sell their wares and for artisans to showcase their skills. The shared experience of the festival fostered a sense of collective identity, strengthening the social bonds within and between different communities. The economic impact of these festivals should not be underestimated; they were significant drivers of regional and national prosperity.

Moreover, the festivals served as a crucial mechanism for reinforcing social order and political legitimacy. The pharaoh's participation in these events demonstrated their connection to the divine and underscored their authority. The festivals, orchestrated by the priesthood, helped to maintain social order and cohesion through shared religious experience. The shared experience of the festival reinforced their collective identity as a people united by faith, enhancing the stability of the socio-political structure. The presence of the pharaoh in these events and the rituals carried out emphasized his or her divinely appointed rule and therefore enhanced social stability.

Beyond the large-scale festivals at Bubastis, smaller, more localized celebrations were held throughout Egypt in Bastet's honor. These localized festivals might have been tied to specific agricultural cycles or local events, emphasizing the goddess's close connection to the everyday lives of ordinary people. These smaller-scale festivals likely included more intimate rituals and community gatherings. The localized celebrations demonstrate the deeply personal aspect of Bastet's worship; she wasn't just a distant, powerful deity; she was also a protector and a source of comfort within the local communities. The smaller festivals highlight the pervasive nature of Bastet's worship, extending her influence beyond the grand scale of large-city celebrations.

The festivals and rituals honoring Bastet weren't merely religious observances; they were integral parts of ancient Egyptian social life. They provided opportunities for social interaction, economic exchange, and the reinforcement of religious beliefs and political power. The joyous celebrations, the solemn rituals, and the sheer scale of these events, as depicted in historical records and revealed through archaeological discoveries, give us a vivid picture of Bastet's enduring influence on ancient Egyptian society. The festivals were powerful forces in shaping the cultural identity and religious practices of ancient Egypt, enriching the daily lives of both the common people and the ruling elite. They provide an invaluable lens through which we can gain a deeper understanding of this ancient civilization and its fascinating religious landscape. The continued study of these festivals, through both textual analysis and archaeological research, promises to unlock further insights into the intricate relationship between religion, society, and daily life in ancient Egypt. These insights allow us to appreciate the enduring power and multifaceted nature of Bastet, the beloved cat goddess.

Bastet in Popular Culture and Literature

Bastet's enduring legacy extends far beyond the sands of ancient Egypt. Her image, imbued with both regal elegance and playful charm, has captivated the imaginations of artists, writers, and filmmakers for centuries, transforming her into a powerful symbol in popular culture and literature. This enduring appeal stems from a potent blend of historical fascination and the inherent allure of the feline form, a creature equally capable of fierce independence and tender affection. However, the modern depictions of Bastet often diverge from the nuanced understanding of her role in ancient Egyptian society, highlighting the complex relationship between historical accuracy and creative interpretation.

One of the most significant ways Bastet has permeated modern culture is through artistic representations. From the meticulously detailed renderings in scholarly publications to the whimsical interpretations in popular art, her image continues to inspire creativity. Early depictions often mirrored the artistic conventions of ancient Egypt, portraying her as a woman with a cat's head, sometimes adorned with regal headdresses and holding symbols of her power, such as the ankh or sistrum. These reproductions, often found in museums and academic texts, strive for historical accuracy, reflecting the stylistic choices of ancient Egyptian artists and the available archaeological evidence. However, modern artists have expanded upon these classic representations, exploring different facets of Bastet's personality and mythology. Some artistic portrayals emphasize her protective nature, depicting her as a fierce warrior goddess, while others focus on her gentler side, portraying her as a nurturing mother or a playful companion. This variety reflects the multifaceted nature of her character as seen through different cultural and individual lenses.

The visual arts aren't the only medium through which Bastet's image has become prominent. She has also found her way into literature, appearing in novels, short stories, and even poems. Her presence in fictional works serves multiple purposes. Sometimes she's a central figure, with narratives that attempt to bring to life her myths and legends, often exploring new aspects of her personality and her relationships with other Egyptian deities. These fictional narratives provide opportunities for creative reinterpretation of the historical record, enriching her mythology with imagined stories and relationships that would otherwise remain lost to history. In other instances, she is incorporated into stories as a minor character or symbol, providing a recognizable element of ancient Egyptian culture that lends authenticity or intrigue to the broader narrative. These appearances, even fleeting ones, contribute to her continued visibility and influence on the public imagination. In some modern fictional works, Bastet's attributes as a protector, a goddess of fertility, and a bringer of joy are emphasized. These reimagining's may diverge significantly from the archaeological record and ancient texts, but they contribute to the collective understanding of her character in modern culture.

The influence of Bastet in popular culture extends beyond the traditional forms of art and literature. Her image has been adopted by various subcultures, from Wiccans and Pagans to fans of fantasy and mythology. These groups may not necessarily adhere to a strictly historical interpretation of Bastet's mythology but they engage with her symbolic representation. For example, she is sometimes invoked in rituals or spell work, signifying aspects of protection, feline grace, feminine power, or connection to nature. Her representation in video games, comic books, and role-playing games further showcases her adaptability as a symbol and her lasting appeal to a broad audience. In these contexts, Bastet often acts as an archetypal character, representing the power of the feminine, the connection between nature and spirituality, or the protective aspects of motherly love. These diverse representations often blend the historical aspects of her mythology with modern elements and sensibilities, highlighting her capacity to resonate with contemporary culture.

It's crucial to acknowledge the difference between accurate historical depictions of Bastet and the creative liberties taken by modern artists and writers. While some works strive for

authenticity, meticulously researching the historical evidence and incorporating ancient texts into their narratives, others prioritize artistic expression or storytelling over historical fidelity. There is a vast difference between a scholarly publication using an image of Bastet based on ancient artifacts and a fictional story in which Bastet has superpowers or engages in actions that completely deviate from her historical background. Understanding this distinction allows viewers and readers to appreciate the value of both approaches. Scholars and enthusiasts of ancient Egyptian history benefit from the historically accurate portrayals that help educate the public, while creative works provide imaginative retellings and interpretations that expand the mythos of the goddess.

However, the modern interpretation of Bastet is not without its pitfalls. The simplification of her complex mythology can lead to misunderstandings and misrepresentations. Reducing her to a mere "cat goddess" ignores the richness and complexity of her association with warfare, protection, and healing. Similarly, romanticizing her image can obscure the historical context in which her worship flourished. While her connection to cats is undeniable, this is only one aspect of her multi-faceted nature. Overemphasis on the feline aspect can trivialize her broader significance in ancient Egyptian society and the intricate role she played in daily life. Her presence in ancient festivals, her association with fertility, and her role as protector of the home all contribute to a richer and deeper understanding of Bastet's complex character.

The appropriation of Bastet's image by some contemporary movements, particularly those related to paganism or witchcraft, can also lead to concerns about cultural sensitivity and responsible representation. It is imperative to respect the historical context of Bastet's worship and avoid misrepresenting or appropriating her image for purposes that might contradict or distort her original significance. Careful research and sensitivity towards the origins of her worship are crucial when engaging with her legacy in contemporary practices. Using her image without a thorough understanding of her cultural roots can lead to misinterpretations and a diluted understanding of her significance within the broader context of ancient Egyptian culture.

Therefore, a careful examination of Bastet's presence in popular culture demands a balanced approach. We should appreciate the creative interpretations and artistic explorations that expand her mythos while maintaining a critical eye towards historical accuracy. It's important to distinguish between creative license and potentially misleading or disrespectful representations. Responsible engagement with Bastet's image and mythology necessitates a keen awareness of historical context and a commitment to accurate representation whenever possible.

The continued fascination with Bastet in modern culture highlights the enduring power of ancient Egyptian mythology and the timeless appeal of the feline form. Her image, imbued with both grace and power, serves as a powerful reminder of the richness and complexity of ancient Egyptian culture. As long as the goddess' image continues to appear in various artistic, literary, and cultural expressions, future generations will continue to explore and reinterpret her mythos, ensuring that Bastet's legacy remains a vibrant and engaging part of our collective imagination. Her story serves as an excellent illustration of how historical figures and myths can transcend time and adapt to contemporary interpretations, highlighting the power of mythology to shape our understanding of the past and inform our views of the present.

The ongoing fascination with Bastet demonstrates the enduring power of ancient mythology to captivate and inspire, encouraging a deeper appreciation of the ancient world and the enduring appeal of its rich tapestry of beliefs and symbols. Her legacy underscores the importance of careful consideration when engaging with historical figures and cultural symbols, ensuring their representation reflects both their historical context and contemporary values.

Cats in Tomb Paintings and Reliefs

Chapter Three

The meticulous artistry of ancient Egyptian tomb paintings and reliefs offers a unique window into the lives and beliefs of their creators. Nowhere is this more evident than in the numerous depictions of cats, which appear across a wide range of contexts, revealing much about their multifaceted role in ancient Egyptian society, both in life and death. These depictions, far from being mere artistic flourishes, provide invaluable insights into the deep-seated reverence and practical importance cats held within this ancient civilization.

One of the most common portrayals of cats in tomb art features them in hunting scenes. These scenes, often vibrant and dynamic, depict cats, typically domestic shorthairs, skillfully pursuing and capturing various prey, such as birds, rodents, and reptiles. These depictions aren't simply realistic representations of feline hunting prowess; they also reflect the practical role cats played in controlling vermin within Egyptian homes and agricultural settings. The efficient pest control provided by cats was undoubtedly highly valued, contributing to their elevated status within society. The skill and precision with which the cats are depicted, often capturing the subtle movements and expressions of a successful hunt, speak to the high regard in which these animals were held and the artists' deep understanding of feline behavior. Variations in the hunting scenes can be noted across different regions and time periods. For instance, tomb paintings from Thebes might depict cats hunting in the lush fields surrounding the Nile, while those from the Delta region might showcase hunting in more arid or marshy environments, reflecting the local ecology. The specific types of prey also differ, reflecting the local fauna. The consistent theme, however, is the portrayal of the cat as a highly capable and efficient hunter, a valuable asset to the household and community.

Beyond their practical contributions, tomb paintings and reliefs also frequently depict cats within the context of religious rituals and ceremonies. Cats associated with the goddess Bastet, naturally, are particularly prevalent. These portrayals often show cats participating in or observing religious acts, highlighting their sacred status. Depictions of cats receiving offerings, being adorned with collars and other adornments, or participating in processions alongside human participants, underscore their role as intermediaries between the human and divine worlds. The careful rendering of these scenes, often with intricate details of the rituals and the accompanying paraphernalia, indicates a strong link between cats and the religious beliefs of the ancient Egyptians. The stylistic choices employed – the use of particular colors, the positioning of the cat within the scene, and the overall composition – all contribute to a powerful visual narrative that emphasizes the religious significance of cats. The consistent presence of cats in these depictions across different periods and locations suggests the pervasive influence of feline deities and the enduring importance of cats within the religious landscape of ancient Egypt.

Another important context for cat depictions is within domestic scenes. Tomb paintings often portray cats relaxing in the homes of the deceased, playfully interacting with children, or simply resting peacefully. These depictions provide a glimpse into the everyday lives of cats as cherished companions and members of the household. The intimacy and affection suggested in these scenes underscore the bond between humans and cats. It's important to note that these representations of domestic cats are not idealized or romanticized; they portray cats as they were—sometimes playful, sometimes indolent, but always present within the everyday domestic space. The level of detail in these depictions, the textures of the cat's fur, the nuances of their expressions—reflects the artists' close observation of feline behavior and suggests the deep affection and respect held for their feline companions. The consistency of these depictions in tombs across different periods and social classes suggests the widespread practice of keeping cats as pets and their acceptance within the household. The inclusion of cats in these intimate scenes provides a powerful counterpoint to their religious and symbolic representations, revealing the multifaceted role they occupied in the daily lives of the ancient Egyptians.

The portrayal of cats in the afterlife is equally fascinating. Tomb paintings often depict cats accompanying the deceased into the next world, suggesting a belief in their role as protectors or guides in the journey to the afterlife. Cats are sometimes shown in scenes of judgment or weighing of the heart, implying their involvement in the assessment of the deceased's moral worthiness. These scenes underscore the close relationship between the living and the dead, and the persistence of the bond between humans and their beloved feline companions beyond the earthly realm. The stylistic conventions used in these scenes, often employing symbolic imagery and iconography associated with the afterlife, reinforce the religious significance of cats and their continued relevance in the transition to the next world. Regional variations in the depiction of cats in the afterlife are less pronounced than in other contexts, suggesting a widespread and uniform belief about the cat's role in the realm of the dead. The consistent appearance of cats in these scenes demonstrates the enduring belief in their mystical powers and their ability to bridge the gap between the living and the dead.

The stylistic variations in the depiction of cats across different periods and regions offer further insights into the evolution of Egyptian art and the changing cultural perceptions of these animals. Earlier dynastic periods might show a more stylized and less realistic representation of cats, reflecting a different artistic tradition. Later periods saw a more naturalistic and detailed depiction, potentially reflecting a growing awareness of feline anatomy and behavior. Regional variations also exist; artists from Thebes, for example, might adopt slightly different stylistic conventions compared to those from Memphis or

Saqqara. These subtle variations are a testament to the dynamic nature of Egyptian art and the adaptability of artistic styles to reflect local influences and individual preferences. Analyzing these stylistic changes allows for a better understanding of the evolution of artistic techniques and the concurrent shifts in cultural attitudes and beliefs towards cats. The attention to detail in even seemingly minor aspects of these depictions – the color of the fur, the positioning of the body, the expression in the eyes – demonstrate the high skill and artistic sensibilities of the ancient Egyptian painters and sculptors. The study of these stylistic nuances offers a rich tapestry of cultural and artistic expressions, all centered around the beloved feline companion.

Examining the prevalence of cats in specific tomb complexes also provides valuable contextual information. The tombs of wealthy individuals and high-ranking officials often feature a larger number and more elaborate depictions of cats than those of commoners. This disparity reflects the social status of the deceased and the resources available to their families for creating their final resting place. The difference in the size, quality, and artistic detail of the feline depictions underscores the social hierarchies within ancient Egyptian society and their influence on funerary practices. However, even in the tombs of commoners, the presence of cat imagery, however modest, testifies to the widespread reverence for these animals across all social strata. The careful analysis of cat depictions in different tomb complexes illuminates the social and economic factors influencing funerary practices and reinforces the universal respect for cats within ancient Egyptian culture.

In conclusion, the abundant portrayal of cats in ancient Egyptian tomb paintings and reliefs offers a rich and multifaceted insight into the animal's significant role in this ancient civilization. From their practical use in hunting vermin to their profound religious significance and the affectionate companionship they provided within the household, the depictions showcase a complex relationship between humans and cats that extended beyond the realm of the living and into the afterlife. The stylistic variations, regional differences, and variations based on the social status of the deceased all offer further avenues for exploring the diverse beliefs, practices, and artistic expressions surrounding cats within ancient Egyptian culture. The continued study of these artistic representations promises to further enrich our understanding of the deep and enduring bond between humans and cats in ancient Egypt.

Cats in Sculpture and Statuary

Beyond the vibrant world of tomb paintings and reliefs, the ancient Egyptians expressed their profound reverence for cats through an extensive array of sculptures and statuary. These three-dimensional representations, ranging from small, intricately carved figurines to monumental statues of the feline goddess Bastet, offer a tangible connection to the beliefs and practices of this ancient civilization. The materials employed, the stylistic choices, and the contexts in which these sculptures were found all contribute to a richer understanding of the multifaceted role cats played in ancient Egyptian life.

One of the most common forms of feline representation in sculpture is the small figurine. These were crafted from a variety of materials, including faience, wood, bronze, and even precious stones like carnelian and lapis lazuli. Faience, a glazed ceramic, was particularly popular, allowing for mass production of relatively inexpensive yet visually appealing figurines. These small sculptures often depict cats in a variety of poses, from the graceful elegance of a seated cat to the dynamic energy of a cat in mid-stride. Some figurines are highly stylized, reflecting the artistic conventions of a particular period or region, while others strive for a greater degree of realism. These variations provide valuable insights into the evolution of sculptural techniques and artistic preferences over time. The presence of these small figurines in tombs, homes, and even everyday settings suggests their widespread popularity as amulets, votive offerings, or simply cherished possessions. The meticulous detail, even in the smallest figurines, speaks to the care and respect with which these objects were created. Detailed examination often reveals intricate markings, including hieroglyphs, suggesting a possible connection to specific deities, spells or even the owner of the figurine.

The sheer number of surviving cat figurines discovered at archaeological sites—ranging from simple, almost mass-produced examples to extraordinarily detailed and elaborately decorated pieces—attests to the enduring popularity of these objects. The differences in materials, stylistic choices, and level of detail highlight not only the artistic skill of the artisans but also the varying economic means of those who owned them. A careful study of these figurines allows us to reconstruct the social landscape of ancient Egypt, demonstrating that the veneration of cats transcended social class and economic status. Even modest figurines, crafted from readily available materials, demonstrate a profound respect for the feline form and its associated symbolism. Moreover, the discovery of figurines in contexts far removed from elite burials suggests that the association with cats extended to everyday life, further demonstrating the significant role they played in ancient Egyptian society.

Beyond the small figurines, monumental statues of Bastet, the cat goddess, represent a significant body of ancient Egyptian sculptural art. These statues, often crafted from stone, wood, or metal, vary dramatically in size and style, reflecting different artistic conventions and regional influences. Smaller statues, suitable for domestic shrines or temple offerings, might depict Bastet in a more intimate and personal scale, showcasing her nurturing and protective aspects. Larger statues, intended for public display in temples or significant public spaces, frequently present Bastet in a more regal and powerful manner, emphasizing her authority and divine status. These monumental sculptures often feature highly stylized details, such as intricate headdresses, jewelry, and other symbolic attributes, further emphasizing Bastet's complex nature and divine power. The materials employed were often chosen to reflect the goddess's attributes; for instance, gold, a precious metal associated with the sun and divinity, was often used for smaller, more personal depictions.

Some notable examples of Bastet statuary highlight the artistic sophistication of ancient Egyptian sculptors. Certain statues, found in significant temple complexes, showcase remarkably lifelike representations of Bastet, with a level of detail and anatomical accuracy that is striking. These statues not only convey the feline features with precision but also capture a sense of grace and majesty. The careful rendering of the fur, the subtle curves of the body, and the expressive eyes all contribute to a powerfully evocative image of the goddess.

Other examples, especially those from later periods, might show a more stylized representation, emphasizing symbolic elements over anatomical accuracy. These stylistic variations across time and location provide crucial insights into the changing cultural perceptions of Bastet and the evolution of artistic conventions. The study of these sculptures enables us to trace the changing artistic preferences and religious interpretations across different periods of ancient Egyptian history.

Beyond statues of Bastet herself, other feline-related sculptures exist, illustrating the broader importance of cats in ancient Egyptian religion and culture. Some sculptures depict cats in conjunction with other deities, such as Sekhmet, another powerful feline goddess associated with protection and warfare. These depictions illuminate the interconnectedness of various deities and their shared feline associations. Other sculptures feature cats in symbolic roles, such as guardians or protectors of the deceased. These often appear in funerary contexts, acting as a visual representation of the watchful protection offered by these revered animals in the afterlife. Furthermore, some sculptures might depict cats engaging in everyday activities, such as hunting or playing, providing a tangible reminder of the intimate bond between humans and cats within ancient Egyptian society. These sculptures frequently serve as a powerful symbol of the relationship between humans and their feline companions.

The materials used in creating these sculptures also reveal important information about their intended purpose and the cultural significance of the cats themselves. Precious materials, such as gold, silver, or semi-precious stones, suggest that the sculpture was associated with important religious contexts or high-status individuals. The use of such materials reinforces the sacred and revered status of cats and the goddess Bastet. More commonplace materials, like wood or faience, suggest a broader distribution of feline imagery, indicating that the veneration of cats was a widespread practice across different social strata. The choice of materials directly reflects the intended function and symbolic meaning of the sculpture. Careful study of the materials and construction techniques used allows for greater understanding of the social, economic, and religious factors that influenced the creation and use of these sculptures.

In conclusion, the sculptural representations of cats in ancient Egypt provide a rich tapestry of information concerning the profound relationship between humans and felines in this ancient civilization. From the mass-produced figurines to the monumental statues of Bastet, these three-dimensional representations reveal not only the artistic skill of the ancient Egyptian sculptors but also the deep religious and cultural significance of cats within their society. The stylistic variations, the materials employed, and the contexts in which these sculptures were found offer invaluable insights into the complexities of ancient Egyptian beliefs and practices. The continuing study of these sculptures promises to further enrich our understanding of the enduring legacy of cats in the rich history of ancient Egypt. The careful analysis of these sculptures, combined with other archaeological findings and textual evidence, allows for a more complete and nuanced understanding of the revered status cats occupied in ancient Egypt. The enduring appeal of these artistic representations—a testament to the enduring fascination with the relationship between humanity and the feline world—continues to intrigue and inspire us today.

Cats in Amulets and Jewelry

Beyond the grand statues and elaborate tomb paintings, the reverence for cats in ancient Egypt is perhaps most intimately revealed through the widespread use of feline imagery in amulets and jewelry. These personal adornments, often worn daily, served not only as decorative items but also as powerful talismans, imbued with protective and magical properties. Their prevalence across social strata underscores the deeply ingrained belief in the cat's mystical connection to the divine and the unseen world.

The materials used in creating these cat amulets and jewelry varied widely, reflecting both the wearer's status and the intended purpose of the piece. Precious metals, such as gold and silver, were favored for amulets intended for high-ranking individuals or religious contexts. Gold, in particular, held significant symbolic weight, associated with the sun god Ra and representing divine power and immortality. Elaborate gold cat amulets, often intricately detailed and adorned with precious stones, have been found in elite tombs, indicating their association with the deceased's journey into the afterlife. These amulets were often inscribed with protective spells or the names of protective deities, further reinforcing their magical efficacy.

Silver, while less expensive than gold, was still a highly valued metal, carrying its own symbolic weight. Silver cat amulets, while perhaps less lavishly decorated than their gold counterparts, were still significant items, often featuring intricate designs and detailed representations of cats in various poses. The use of silver suggests that access to these protective amulets extended beyond the elite, although the quality of the craftsmanship and the embellishments could vary widely depending on the wearer's social standing.

Beyond precious metals, a vast array of other materials were employed in the creation of cat amulets and jewelry. Faience, a vibrant glazed ceramic, was exceptionally popular due to its versatility and affordability. Faience cat amulets were produced in large quantities, allowing for widespread distribution and access across social classes. The bright colors and intricate designs of these amulets made them highly appealing, even though the material itself held less inherent value than gold or silver. The variety of colors and designs available within faience amulets suggest a wide range of symbolic meanings and potential associations with specific deities or protective spells.

Other materials, such as carnelian, lapis lazuli, and other semi-precious stones, were frequently used in the creation of cat amulets and jewelry. These stones, with their own associated symbolic meanings, further enhanced the magical and protective qualities attributed to the amulets. Carnelian, for instance, was often linked to life and regeneration, making it a particularly appropriate choice for amulets associated with protection and the afterlife. Lapis lazuli, with its deep blue hue, was associated with divinity and royalty, bestowing an air of prestige and power upon the amulets in which it featured.

The forms and styles of cat amulets and jewelry were equally diverse, reflecting stylistic changes over time and regional variations in artistic preferences. Some amulets depict cats in a highly stylized manner, emphasizing symbolic features over realistic representation. These stylized amulets often featured simplified forms, focusing on key elements such as the feline head or body, enhancing their mystical properties. Other amulets, particularly those made of precious metals or semi-precious stones, strived for a higher degree of realism, capturing the grace and elegance of the feline form. The degree of realism often correlates with the value of the material used and the social status of the owner.

Certain common motifs occur frequently in cat amulets and jewelry. The seated cat, often depicted with a serene and dignified demeanor, was a popular choice, signifying protection, stability, and domestic tranquility. The nursing cat, a powerful symbol of motherhood and nurturing, frequently appeared as amulets to promote fertility and prosperity. The cat in mid-

stride, dynamic and alert, represented the fierce protective power of the cat and its association with the goddess Sekhmet. The cat's head, a simpler yet equally potent form, could stand on its own as an amulet, its powerful presence offering protection against harm and misfortune. The choice of motif likely reflects the wearer's personal needs and aspirations, choosing an amulet that resonated with their specific concerns.

The inscriptions found on some cat amulets and jewelry further enhance our understanding of their magical properties. Many amulets feature hieroglyphic inscriptions, including protective spells, the names of deities, or personal invocations. These inscriptions not only add a layer of personalized meaning to the amulet but also provide invaluable insights into ancient Egyptian magical practices and beliefs. The spells inscribed on the amulets often invoke the power of specific deities, such as Bastet, Sekhmet, or Mafdet, seeking their protection and intervention. The inclusion of personal names or wishes suggests that the amulets were not merely generic talismans but were tailored to the specific needs and desires of their owners.

The discovery of cat amulets and jewelry in various archaeological contexts provides additional context for their use and significance. These artifacts are often found in tombs, alongside other funerary goods, suggesting their role in protecting the deceased in the afterlife. The presence of these amulets in everyday settings, however, demonstrates that they were not solely associated with death and the underworld but were also considered potent tools for protection and well-being in life. Their presence in both sacred and secular contexts highlights the multifaceted nature of their magical significance, emphasizing the importance of feline protection in all aspects of life.

In conclusion, the cat amulets and jewelry of ancient Egypt reveal a profound and complex relationship between humans and cats, extending far beyond simple companionship. These small but significant artifacts serve as tangible manifestations of the deep-seated belief in the cat's spiritual power and its ability to protect and guide individuals through both life and the afterlife. The diverse materials, forms, and inscriptions found on these amulets provide invaluable insights into ancient Egyptian religious practices, magical beliefs, and the enduring reverence for the feline form. The continued study of these artifacts allows for a deeper understanding of the profound significance cats held in the lives of the ancient Egyptians and their lasting legacy within the rich tapestry of ancient Egyptian culture. Their continued fascination today speaks volumes of the enduring mystery and power associated with the cat in ancient Egyptian belief. The study of these small objects offers a captivating glimpse into the rich world of ancient Egyptian spirituality and the profound reverence held for the feline form.

Architectural Representations of Cats

The pervasive reverence for cats in ancient Egypt extended beyond personal adornments and into the very fabric of their architectural landscape. Feline imagery, subtly woven into the design of temples, palaces, and other significant structures, served not merely as decorative elements but as powerful symbols reflecting the profound beliefs and cosmological understandings of the ancient Egyptians. The strategic placement of these images within the architectural context speaks volumes about their intended purpose and symbolic resonance.

Temples dedicated to feline goddesses, such as Bastet in Bubastis and Sekhmet in Memphis, offer the most direct and elaborate examples of architectural cat representations. The Bubastis temple complex, a sprawling site dedicated to Bastet, the gentle lion-headed goddess associated with domestic cats, featured countless depictions of felines throughout its structures. These depictions ranged from intricate relief carvings of Bastet herself, often depicted seated and nursing kittens, to smaller, more subtle representations of cats integrated into architectural details. The scale and frequency of these images emphasized Bastet's central role in the lives of the ancient Egyptians and the temple's function as a nexus of religious devotion. The placement of feline imagery, particularly those of Bastet, within the innermost sanctuaries and along processional pathways, suggests that they were intended to guide and protect worshippers as they approached the divine presence. This careful orchestration of visual cues transformed the architectural space itself into a powerful expression of religious faith.

Similarly, the temples dedicated to Sekhmet, the fearsome lion-headed goddess of war and protection, prominently featured feline imagery, although the aesthetic and symbolic connotations differed significantly from those found in Bastet's temples. Sekhmet's temples, often characterized by a more imposing and austere architectural style, employed feline imagery to convey the goddess's formidable power and unwavering protection. Sculptures and reliefs depicting Sekhmet in her ferocious lioness form dominated many of these structures, acting as potent visual reminders of her strength and ability to vanquish evil. The strategic placement of these images, often near entrances or within protective enclosures, reinforces their intended purpose as guardians against malevolent forces. The contrasting styles between Bastet's and Sekhmet's temples reveal the nuanced understanding of feline symbolism within ancient Egyptian religious practices, demonstrating the adaptability and multifaceted nature of feline deities and their representation in architecture.

Beyond temples dedicated specifically to feline goddesses, feline motifs appear frequently in other architectural structures, underscoring their broader cultural significance. Palace reliefs, for instance, often depict cats engaged in various activities, ranging from hunting to playful interactions with humans. These depictions, often integrated seamlessly into narrative scenes, suggest that cats held a respected position within royal households and enjoyed a level of familiarity and companionship that extended beyond the religious sphere. The inclusion of feline imagery within palace architecture speaks to their elevated status and the appreciation of their beauty and grace within the royal court. These portrayals often contrast with the stylized religious depictions found in temples, reflecting a different aspect of the cat's role in ancient Egyptian society.

The use of feline motifs in less prominent architectural elements further demonstrates the pervasive nature of their symbolic significance. Minor architectural features, such as capitals, columns, and decorative friezes, frequently incorporate stylized feline forms. These subtle yet pervasive representations served to subtly infuse the architectural space with feline symbolism, subtly reminding inhabitants and visitors alike of the power and grace of the feline form. This consistent integration of feline imagery, even in seemingly insignificant details, reinforces its deeply ingrained presence within ancient Egyptian culture and daily life. The artistry and

precision evident in these details further highlight the importance and the care invested in their creation, indicating their symbolic significance.

The materials used in the creation of architectural feline imagery also hold symbolic weight. The use of precious materials such as gold, silver, or intricately painted limestone for representations of feline deities like Bastet or Sekhmet emphasizes their divine status and association with power, immortality, and the realm of the gods. The use of simpler materials like faience or painted stucco in domestic or less sacred settings indicates a more general appreciation for feline imagery and its incorporation into daily life. The craftsmanship involved in the creation of these representations often reached extraordinary levels of skill, indicating the care taken to render these images as accurately and symbolically powerful as possible. The varying levels of detail, depending on the location and purpose of the image, also hint at the nuanced understanding of feline symbolism and its application within different contexts.

The study of architectural feline representations also reveals stylistic changes and regional variations. While stylistic conventions varied across different periods and geographic regions, the recurring presence of feline motifs throughout the long history of ancient Egypt underscores the enduring cultural significance of cats. The changes in artistic styles, from the more stylized representations of the Early Dynastic Period to the more naturalistic depictions of later periods, reflect the evolution of artistic techniques and aesthetic preferences, yet the enduring symbolism of the feline form remains consistent. The comparison of feline depictions in different temples and palaces across Egypt highlights regional differences in artistic styles and cultural practices, providing valuable insights into the diverse aspects of ancient Egyptian culture.

Examining the placement of feline representations in relation to other architectural and symbolic elements within a given structure further reveals their significance. For instance, the placement of feline images near entrances might signify protection or guardianship, whereas their presence within inner sanctuaries could indicate a connection to the sacred space or to specific deities. The proximity of feline images to other religious symbols, such as sun disks or hieroglyphs, can provide additional clues to their intended meaning and function. A careful analysis of these relationships allows for a more nuanced understanding of the role feline imagery played within the wider symbolic system of ancient Egyptian architecture.

The continued excavation and study of ancient Egyptian architectural sites provide ever-increasing opportunities to discover and understand the architectural representations of cats. New discoveries regularly shed light on previously unknown aspects of ancient Egyptian beliefs and practices, continually enriching our understanding of the profound connection between humans and felines in ancient Egypt. The ongoing research and analysis of architectural feline representations promise to further illuminate the complex web of beliefs, practices, and cultural values associated with cats in ancient Egypt. This research emphasizes not just the visual representations, but also the contextual significance within the overall architectural plan and its associated religious or social functions.

In conclusion, the architectural representations of cats in ancient Egypt go beyond mere decoration; they constitute a powerful visual language reflecting the deep-seated reverence and complex symbolism associated with felines. Their presence in temples, palaces, and other structures across diverse periods and regions underscores the enduring significance of cats within ancient Egyptian society, and the rich tapestry of beliefs and practices woven into their cultural fabric. The strategic placement, material choices, and stylistic variations of these images offer invaluable insights into ancient Egyptian religious beliefs, royal power, social structures, and artistic expressions, underscoring the profound and multifaceted nature of the human-feline relationship in ancient Egypt. The ongoing study of these architectural elements continually reveals new aspects of this fascinating connection, continuing to enrich our understanding of this remarkable civilization.

The Symbolic Meaning of Cats in Art

The symbolic meaning of cats in ancient Egyptian art extends far beyond simple depictions of the animals themselves. Their representation in art became a powerful and multifaceted language, conveying complex religious, social, and cosmological ideas. The choice of pose, color, materials, and the context within which cats were depicted all contributed to their nuanced symbolic meaning. Understanding this symbolism requires a careful examination of the artistic conventions employed by ancient Egyptian artists and the cultural beliefs that underpinned their work.

One of the most fundamental aspects of feline symbolism lies in the association of cats with specific deities. Bastet, the lioness-headed goddess of protection, joy, and fertility, is perhaps the most readily associated feline deity. Depictions of Bastet often show her as a serene, seated lioness, sometimes nursing kittens, emphasizing her nurturing and protective aspects. The use of specific colors, such as gold or a specific shade of red, further enhanced these symbolic connotations, linking her with the sun, warmth, and life-giving energy. However, the representation of Bastet could also be fierce and powerful, reflecting the dual nature of her protective capabilities. This duality mirrored the complex beliefs about the balance of opposing forces within the ancient Egyptian worldview. Representations of Bastet in art frequently emphasized her protective role, safeguarding individuals, communities, and even the pharaoh himself. In some instances, she was depicted wielding weapons or in battle scenes, reflecting her ability to vanquish evil.

In contrast to Bastet's often serene image, Sekhmet, the fierce lion-headed goddess of war and destruction, was depicted in a far more aggressive manner. Her representations typically showed her as a powerful, imposing lioness, often roaring or with bared teeth, underscoring her formidable strength and ability to punish those who defied the divine order. The materials used in sculpting or painting Sekhmet often reinforced this image of power, with the use of hard stones like granite or basalt conveying her strength and unwavering nature. Her presence in art served as a potent reminder of divine justice and the need for maintaining Ma'at, the cosmic order. The contrast between Bastet and Sekhmet's artistic representations demonstrates the subtle but significant ways in which ancient Egyptians conveyed diverse aspects of their deities through symbolic imagery.

Beyond the major feline goddesses, cats also appeared in art associated with other deities and mythological narratives. They often featured in scenes depicting the funerary rituals and beliefs related to the afterlife. Cats were sometimes included in scenes showing the weighing of the heart ceremony, a pivotal moment in the judgment of the deceased. Their presence may have signified the soul's journey into the next life or the protection of the deceased during their transition. In other instances, cats were linked to deities associated with specific aspects of the natural world, for instance, cats were connected to the sun god Ra, perhaps due to the cat's association with solar energy, warmth, and regeneration. This connection manifested in the use of feline imagery in sun temples and funerary texts.

The artistic representation of cats also varied based on the medium used. Wall paintings, sculptures, amulets, and other forms of artwork depicted cats in different styles, sometimes realistically and at other times in a more stylized or symbolic form. The level of detail and realism often depended on the artistic context and the purpose of the artwork. For instance, the cats depicted in tomb paintings often possess a more naturalistic appearance, reflecting the everyday life of the time. The context suggests a more informal setting, showing the connection between humans and animals in their daily lives. However, statues and amulets often used stylized representations of cats, highlighting specific aspects of their symbolic meaning. The materials used also impacted the symbolic meaning. The use of precious materials such as gold, lapis lazuli, and semi-precious stones often indicated the sacred or divine nature of the feline representation, underlining the close relationship between cats and the realm of gods.

The use of common materials such as wood, faience, or clay might indicate a more utilitarian purpose or a representation of domestic cats.

The poses and actions of cats in ancient Egyptian art also played a significant role in conveying their symbolic meaning. Cats depicted in hunting scenes, often capturing birds or snakes, symbolized their inherent skills and association with protection. Similarly, the act of nursing kittens signified the life-giving power and nurturing aspect of cats, particularly connected with the goddess Bastet. Cats depicted in a playful or affectionate manner emphasized their companionship and their integrated place within the household. However, even these seemingly simple depictions can convey deeper meanings when considered within the context of the surrounding imagery and the overall message of the artwork. The placement of feline imagery within larger narrative scenes provides further insights into the function and intended meaning of the feline representation.

Furthermore, the size and scale of cat representations also influenced their symbolic significance. Large-scale sculptures of feline goddesses emphasized their divine power and influence. Smaller representations, such as amulets and decorative items, served as personal talismans or expressions of devotion. These differences in scale further highlighted the multifaceted nature of feline symbolism in ancient Egyptian art. The varied sizes and levels of detail indicated different functions within society, religious settings, and personal lives.

The study of cat representations in ancient Egyptian art demonstrates the intricate interplay between artistic conventions and cultural beliefs. Ancient Egyptian artists skillfully employed a range of techniques to convey the profound symbolism associated with cats. The use of colors, materials, poses, and context combined to create a rich and multifaceted language that conveyed a deeper understanding of the ancient Egyptian worldview. This symbolic language continues to fascinate and inspire scholars and artists today, revealing the enduring power of feline symbolism in ancient Egyptian culture. By studying these artistic representations, we can uncover a deeper understanding of the profound connection between humans and felines in ancient Egypt, a connection that has left its mark on history and continues to resonate with us today.

The continued exploration and analysis of ancient Egyptian art promise to further reveal the intricacies of feline symbolism. New discoveries and advances in research methods continually enhance our understanding of the cultural beliefs that informed the artistic representations of cats. As we continue to study the rich legacy of ancient Egyptian art, we are reminded of the lasting influence of feline symbolism on the civilization's cultural landscape. The depth and complexity of this symbolism offer valuable insights into the ancient Egyptian worldview, underscoring the multifaceted nature of their relationship with the feline world and highlighting the importance of cats in their religious, social, and daily lives. The enduring fascination with these artistic representations continues to fuel research and inspire further exploration into this fascinating aspect of ancient Egyptian culture.

Mummified Cats and Their Burial Practices

Chapter Four

The reverence afforded to cats in ancient Egypt transcended mere adoration; it extended to their afterlife, culminating in the widespread practice of mummification. Unlike the elaborate mummification processes reserved for pharaohs and the elite, feline mummification varied in complexity depending on the cat's perceived status and the owner's resources. Archaeological excavations, particularly at sites like Beni Hasan and Tuna el-Gebel, have yielded astonishing quantities of mummified cats, testament to the scale of this practice. These discoveries provide invaluable insights into the methods, motivations, and societal implications of this unique funerary ritual.

The mummification process for cats, while simpler than that employed for humans, still involved several key steps. Initially, the cat's body was eviscerated, though the extent of this process varied. Some mummies show evidence of only minimal evisceration, while others indicate a more thorough removal of internal organs. This variation likely reflects economic factors and the perceived importance of the individual cat. Following evisceration, the body cavity was often packed with natron, a naturally occurring salt mixture with desiccant properties, accelerating the drying process and preventing decomposition. The body was then wrapped in linen bandages, sometimes adorned with amulets or other decorative elements, and placed within a simple coffin or cartonnage, a type of papier-mâché casing. The quality of the materials used, the intricacy of the wrapping, and the presence of amulets all reflected the cat's status and the devotion of its owner.

The types of cats mummified also reveal important aspects of their relationship with humans. While domestic cats were the most commonly mummified, depictions and mummified remains also reveal the presence of wild cats like servals and even lions, though these were less frequent. The mummification of wild cats highlights the ancient Egyptians' broader respect for felines beyond the confines of the domestic sphere. These mummified animals often received less elaborate treatment compared to their domestic counterparts, indicating a distinction in their perceived spiritual significance. Furthermore, the size and age of the mummified cats varied considerably, suggesting that cats of all ages and sizes were considered worthy of funerary rituals. The abundance of kitten mummies underscores the special place kittens held within the culture, perhaps symbolizing innocence, rebirth, or the enduring cycle of life.

The sheer number of mummified cats discovered underscores the scale and significance of this practice. Some sites contain vast catacombs specifically dedicated to the burial of cats, hinting at organized funerary rites and potentially professional services dedicated to feline mummification. These cat cemeteries reflect a collective societal effort, signifying the widespread belief in the importance of honoring cats even after death. The scale of these operations suggests the existence of a significant economic enterprise surrounding the mummification and burial of cats, impacting the daily lives of numerous individuals involved in various aspects of this ritual.

The reasons behind the widespread mummification of cats are multifaceted and rooted in the ancient Egyptians' profound religious beliefs. The most prominent factor is the strong association of cats with Bastet, the feline goddess of protection, fertility, and joy. By mummifying cats, the ancient Egyptians may have believed they were honoring Bastet directly, ensuring the continued protection and benevolence of the goddess. This practice could be interpreted as an act of piety, a way of showing devotion and gratitude to a deity closely identified with feline forms. The mummified cats, in a sense, became symbolic representations of Bastet, their afterlife intertwined with her divine power.

Beyond Bastet, the association of cats with other deities, particularly those connected with the sun and the underworld, likely also contributed to the practice of mummification. Cats, often perceived as mediating between the realms of the living and the dead, may have been viewed as guides for the souls navigating the afterlife. The presence of amulets and other ritual objects within the cat mummies lends credence to this interpretation. These amulets may have served as talismans to protect the cat's soul during its journey into the afterlife, ensuring safe passage and a favorable judgment in the Hall of Two Truths.

Moreover, the mummification of beloved pets reflects a deep emotional connection between humans and their feline companions. The effort and resources dedicated to the mummification process indicate a genuine affection and sense of loss, highlighting the importance of cats within the family unit. The carefully wrapped bodies and accompanying burial rites speak volumes about the strong bond shared between ancient Egyptians and their cats, transforming these creatures from mere pets into cherished members of the household. The emotional investment in these funerary rituals is a testament to the cultural significance of the human-feline bond in ancient Egypt.

The practice of cat mummification continued for centuries, reflecting the enduring nature of religious beliefs and the consistent importance attributed to cats throughout ancient Egyptian history. The sheer number of mummified cats discovered across numerous sites underscores the persistent nature of this practice, providing evidence of a deep-rooted societal commitment to this unique funerary tradition. The consistency and pervasiveness of this practice over such an extended period offer profound insight into the steadfastness of ancient Egyptian religious beliefs and their societal impact.

However, the practice wasn't uniform. The quality of mummification varied considerably, suggesting a range of socioeconomic factors influenced the ritual. The wealthier classes could afford more elaborate mummification procedures, while those with fewer resources may have resorted to simpler techniques. This variation reflects social stratification within ancient Egyptian society and the impact of economic factors on religious practices. This unevenness in the treatment of mummified cats offers further insights into the social dynamics and hierarchical structures prevalent within ancient Egyptian society.

Furthermore, the discovery of vast numbers of mummified cats in specific locations led to the speculation about the role of organized religious institutions in managing these large-scale burials. The sheer volume suggests the existence of professional mummifiers specializing in feline mummification, indicating a division of labor within religious practice and potential commercial enterprises associated with the afterlife rituals. The scale of operation suggests a well-organized system involving various individuals contributing to the preparation, burial, and maintenance of these feline cemeteries.

The study of mummified cats continues to reveal new insights into ancient Egyptian culture and religion.

Advances in scientific techniques, such as radiocarbon dating and DNA analysis, are shedding light on the specific types of cats mummified, their ages, and even their diets. This new data helps to refine our understanding of the relationship between ancient Egyptians and their feline companions. The continuous refinement of analytical methods promises further advancements in our knowledge of ancient Egyptian mummification practices.

In conclusion, the mummification of cats in ancient Egypt represents a unique and fascinating aspect of their culture and religious beliefs. The evidence from archaeological discoveries and the analysis of ancient texts illuminate a complex interplay of religious veneration, societal practices, and emotional connections that contributed to this widespread ritual. The sheer scale of cat mummification, the varying degrees of complexity in the process, and the diversity of cats themselves reflect a rich and multifaceted relationship between humans and felines in ancient Egypt, leaving an enduring legacy that continues to fascinate and inform our

understanding of this ancient civilization. Future research promises to further illuminate the depths of this compelling aspect of ancient Egyptian life.

Cat Mummies in Archaeological Contexts

The sheer volume of cat mummies unearthed across Egypt provides unparalleled insight into the ancient

Egyptians' beliefs regarding the afterlife and the profound reverence they held for felines. These weren't isolated incidents of pet burial; rather, they represent a widespread, organized, and potentially commercially driven practice that spanned centuries. The archaeological context of these discoveries is crucial to understanding their significance.

One of the most significant sites for understanding cat mummification is Tuna el-Gebel, located in Upper Egypt. This vast necropolis, sprawling across several hundred acres, is renowned not only for its human burials but also for its extensive cat cemeteries. Excavations at Tuna el-Gebel have yielded tens of thousands of cat mummies, often interred in elaborate shafts and subterranean chambers. The sheer scale of these cemeteries suggests a well-organized system for the collection, preparation, and burial of these animals, possibly involving dedicated priests, embalmers, and even workers specializing in the construction and maintenance of these subterranean burial sites. The layout of the cemeteries, often organized and stratified, hints at a level of social and religious organization far beyond simple individual burials. Detailed studies of the architectural features of these burial complexes reveal that certain areas might have been dedicated to cats of specific ages, breeds, or even social status within the Egyptian society. The variation in the size and complexity of the burial chambers themselves, ranging from simple pits to elaborate structures, further supports the idea of a hierarchal structure within this funerary system for cats. The presence of dedicated burial shafts, indicating a ritualistic process, underscores the societal investment in these feline burials. The careful placement of the mummies and the use of specific materials in their construction also points to a highly structured and regulated process.

Another key location revealing the depth of cat mummification practices is Beni Hasan. Situated in Middle Egypt, this site, primarily known for its rock-cut tombs of nobles from the Middle Kingdom, also contains significant evidence of cat burials. While not on the same scale as Tuna el-Gebel, the presence of cat mummies at Beni Hasan indicates that the practice was not confined to specific geographic regions or social classes. The discovery of cat mummies alongside human burials at Beni Hasan suggests a potential connection between human and feline afterlives, perhaps reflecting beliefs in a shared journey to the underworld or a shared destiny within the larger cosmology. The meticulous arrangement of the cat mummies at Beni Hasan, along with the presence of offerings, suggests a deliberate act of honoring the animals and ensuring their safe passage to the afterlife. These archaeological contexts highlight the pervasiveness and cultural significance of cat veneration throughout different periods and regions of ancient Egypt.

The types of containers used for cat mummies also offer valuable insights into the practice's evolution and the social standing of the feline. Many cat mummies were found entombed in simple linen wrappings, indicating a more basic form of mummification. However, others were encased in elaborate cartonnage coffins, often decorated with vibrant paintings and inscribed with hieroglyphs. The decoration on these cartonnage coffins often depicted the deceased cat in various guises, sometimes as a deity or a representation of Bastet herself. The presence of amulets, such as the wedjat eye, often associated with protection and healing, underscores the belief in their continued spiritual significance even after death. These variations highlight the differing levels of care and resources invested in the mummification process, reflecting a social hierarchy within the practice and perhaps mirroring the social standing of the cat's owner. The materials used in the construction of the coffins, ranging from simple wood to more expensive materials like gilded wood or faience, further emphasize the social stratification within the funerary system. Even the size and condition of the cartonnage coffins serve as indicators of the care given to the mummies, with some showing signs of repair and reuse, indicating a possible recycling of resources within the funerary system.

Further investigations into the context of cat mummies have also revealed the presence of other grave goods alongside the mummies. These offerings, ranging from food and drink to small toys and personal items, indicate that the ancient Egyptians did not see cat mummies as simply discarded remains. They provided them with the essentials required for a comfortable afterlife. The inclusion of such grave goods signifies the profound emotional connection between humans and their feline companions. It suggests that the mummification process wasn't solely a religious practice; it was also an act of remembrance and mourning for beloved pets. The variety of grave goods found with the mummies also illustrates the significance of cats within different social contexts, with some burials showcasing more elaborate and valuable offerings compared to others. The analysis of these offerings provides crucial evidence of the ancient Egyptians' worldview and their understanding of the afterlife.

The archaeological evidence, therefore, paints a vivid picture of a widespread and deeply rooted practice. The sheer scale of cat mummies discovered at sites like Tuna el-Gebel and Beni Hasan suggests a complex network of individuals involved in the process—from those who collected the deceased animals, to the embalmers who prepared the bodies, to the laborers who built and maintained the burial complexes. This points to the existence of an organized and possibly commercially driven funerary industry centered around feline mummification. The practice likely engaged a range of social classes, from those who could afford elaborate cartonnage coffins to those who resorted to simpler burials. This aspect of the archaeological context adds another layer of complexity to the understanding of the social dynamics within ancient Egypt. The variation in the quality of mummification across different sites and even within the same site indicates economic and social inequalities, offering valuable insights into the social structure of ancient Egypt and how it impacted religious practices.

The study of these cat mummies also extends beyond simple burial practices. Recent advancements in scientific techniques, such as radiocarbon dating, DNA analysis, and isotopic studies, have further enriched our understanding of these archaeological discoveries. Radiocarbon dating helps pinpoint the time periods in which these cats lived and were mummified, providing chronological markers for the practice. DNA analysis can identify the specific breeds of cats mummified, revealing variations in feline populations across different eras and regions. Isotopic studies of the cats' bones and teeth can shed light on their diets and overall health, revealing details about their lifecycles and their relationships with humans. The integration of scientific analysis with archaeological data strengthens the interpretation of the social, economic, and religious implications of cat mummification in ancient Egypt. This interdisciplinary approach offers a far more nuanced understanding than previously possible.

In conclusion, the archaeological discoveries of cat mummies, coupled with scientific analysis, provide a rich and multifaceted understanding of ancient Egyptian beliefs about the afterlife, their relationship with cats, and the social and economic structures of their society. The vast cemeteries at Tuna el-Gebel and Beni Hasan, the varying degrees of mummification complexity, the grave goods accompanying the mummies, and the integration of modern scientific techniques all contribute to a comprehensive picture of this remarkable aspect of ancient Egyptian culture. The continued study of cat mummies promises to unveil further insights into the fascinating world of ancient Egypt and its enduring connection with the feline world. The ongoing archaeological research and scientific analysis continues to refine our understanding of these fascinating artifacts and their significance within the broader context of ancient Egyptian society and religion. The enduring legacy of these feline burials highlights the powerful bond between humans and animals in the ancient world, a bond that continues to resonate with us today.

The Role of Cats in the Funerary Rituals

The profound reverence afforded cats in ancient Egypt extended beyond their living lives; it deeply permeated their funerary practices. While the sheer number of mummified cats unearthed across the land speaks volumes about their importance, a closer examination of their role within the funerary rituals reveals a more nuanced understanding of their symbolic significance in the afterlife. The inclusion of cats in burial offerings, for instance, wasn't arbitrary; it stemmed from complex beliefs about their connection to the spiritual realm and their potential to aid the deceased in their journey to the next world.

The offerings found alongside cat mummies vary considerably, reflecting the social status of both the cat and its owner. Simple burials might contain only a few meager items, perhaps a small bowl of food or a simple linen shroud, suggesting the cat may have been a working animal or a less cherished pet. In contrast, more elaborate burials often featured an array of offerings, mirroring the opulence seen in human burials. These could include intricate cartonnage coffins adorned with hieroglyphs and vibrant paintings depicting the cat as a deity or a symbolic representation of Bastet. Precious amulets, such as the wedjat eye, symbolizing protection and healing, were frequently included, emphasizing the continued spiritual significance of the cat even in death. The presence of food and drink offerings, sometimes even toys, reinforces the belief that the cat was expected to continue its existence in the afterlife, requiring sustenance and comfort.

The careful selection and arrangement of these grave goods reveal a degree of ritualistic precision. The positioning of the cat mummy itself, the orientation of the offerings, and even the specific types of food included, all suggest a carefully orchestrated process guided by religious beliefs and funerary customs. The consistent presence of specific items in certain types of cat burials further strengthens the argument for a standardized ritual practice. Detailed analysis of these grave goods offers invaluable insights into the beliefs and practices surrounding cat burials, highlighting the rich tapestry of funerary rituals that intertwined the lives of cats and humans in ancient Egypt.

The association of cats with specific deities of the afterlife further illuminates their role in funerary rituals. Bastet, the cat goddess, was, of course, the most prominent figure, inextricably linked to both the protection of the home and the safe passage of souls to the afterlife. Her presence in funerary contexts is evident through depictions on sarcophagi, amulets, and other grave goods. The image of Bastet, often depicted as a serene cat-headed woman, offered comfort and assurance to the bereaved, signifying the deceased's protection and guidance in the underworld.

Beyond Bastet, other deities associated with the afterlife also had feline connections. Sekhmet, the fierce lion-headed goddess of war and disease, also played a role in funerary rituals, albeit a more ambivalent one. While her ferocious nature could be seen as threatening, she also represented the power of protection and the overcoming of obstacles in the journey to the next world. Her presence in funerary contexts likely signified the successful completion of a dangerous transition. Similarly, Mafdet, the goddess of justice and execution, often depicted as a cat, acted as a protector and guide in the final judgment, ensuring a just and equitable passage into the afterlife.

The symbolic significance of cats in the journey to the next world extended beyond specific deities. The cat's natural agility, independence, and nocturnal habits were linked to the mysteries of the afterlife and the unknown realms beyond. Their ability to see in the dark and their independent nature were viewed as qualities aligning them with the shadowy world of the dead. The cat's association with the sun god Ra, a deity strongly connected with the afterlife, also enhanced their symbolic significance. Cats were believed to share a special connection with the sun, possessing a similar ability to navigate the darkness and transition between realms.

Furthermore, the feline's association with rebirth and regeneration reinforced its importance in funerary rituals. The cat's ability to navigate the shadows and their symbolic link to the sun god Ra further strengthened their association with the cyclical nature of life and death. The mummification of cats, therefore, wasn't merely a preservation of their physical form; it was a ritual reaffirming their journey towards rebirth in the afterlife. The act of mummification itself, echoing the processes applied to humans, symbolized the transformation and continuation of life beyond the physical world.

The prevalence of cat mummies in funerary contexts doesn't only reflect religious beliefs; it reveals a deep emotional connection between ancient Egyptians and their feline companions. The meticulous care taken in preparing the cat mummies, the variety of offerings found in their tombs, and the emotional investment in their burial rituals, all suggest that these animals were valued members of the family, not simply religious symbols. The act of mummifying and burying a cat was a significant act of mourning and a demonstration of love and affection that transcended the boundaries of life and death.

The study of cat mummies also offers valuable insights into the social dynamics of ancient Egyptian society. The differences in the quality and extravagance of cat burials reflect the social hierarchy of the time. Elaborate burials with rich offerings indicate the higher social standing of both the cat's owner and the cat itself, suggesting that certain cats might have been particularly prized or held sacred. The presence of cat mummies in both elite and commoner tombs, however, indicates that the reverence for cats spanned various social classes. The act of burying a beloved pet, irrespective of one's social standing, underscores the shared respect and affection for felines.

The scientific examination of cat mummies has significantly enriched our understanding of their funerary role. Radiocarbon dating, DNA analysis, and isotopic studies provide concrete data about the age, breed, diet, and health of the mummified cats. Such research allows for a more precise understanding of the timeframe in which particular funerary practices were common, and the types of cats involved. By studying cats' diet, we gain insights into their lifestyle and their relationship with humans, adding another dimension to our understanding of the bond between them.

In conclusion, the role of cats in ancient Egyptian funerary rituals was multi-faceted, encompassing religious symbolism, emotional connections, and social dynamics. Their association with deities of the afterlife, their symbolic representation of rebirth and regeneration, and the meticulous care afforded to their mummification and burial, all point to a profound and complex relationship between humans and felines that extended far beyond the boundaries of mortal life. The continued study of these feline burials sheds light not only on ancient Egyptian religious beliefs but also on the rich and complex social tapestry of this fascinating civilization, highlighting the enduring bond between humans and animals that resonates even today. The meticulous care evident in both human and feline burials, alongside the often-lavish grave goods, underscores the widespread belief in the afterlife and the importance of preparing for this journey, regardless of species. The study of cat mummies, therefore, offers a unique window into the beliefs, practices, and emotional lives of the ancient Egyptians, enriching our understanding of this remarkable civilization in a profound way.

Cats as Guides to the Afterlife

The meticulous preparation and elaborate burials of cats in ancient Egypt strongly suggest a belief extending beyond simple veneration; it points to a conviction that these felines played an active role in the afterlife, potentially acting as guides or protectors for the deceased on their journey to the Duat. This hypothesis, while not explicitly stated in a single definitive text, is strongly supported by a confluence of artistic representations, funerary practices, and the symbolic associations imbued upon cats within the broader Egyptian religious framework.

Consider, for example, the numerous depictions of cats within tomb paintings and funerary scenes. These are not merely decorative elements; the careful placement and context within these scenes offer significant clues. Cats are frequently portrayed accompanying the deceased, often depicted near or even within the boat journeys across the perilous waters of the underworld. This visual association immediately suggests a protective or guiding role.

The cat, with its inherent agility and nocturnal prowess, is symbolically positioned to assist the deceased in navigating the treacherous path to the afterlife, potentially warding off malevolent spirits or providing comfort in the face of the unknown. The choice of a cat, rather than any other animal, is significant; its independent nature and ability to see in the dark mirror the perceived challenges and uncertainties of the journey to the Duat, suggesting a creature uniquely suited to the task.

Further evidence arises from the prevalence of cat amulets and figurines within tombs. These weren't just random inclusions; they were carefully selected objects imbued with specific symbolic meaning. The wedjat eye, for instance, a potent amulet frequently found with both human and feline burials, is a powerful symbol of protection and healing. Its presence in cat burials reinforces the idea that the cat itself was considered a protector, its spiritual essence continuing to safeguard the deceased even in the afterlife. Other amulets, depicting deities like Bastet or Sekhmet, further solidified this connection, adding a divine layer of protection to the feline guide. The deliberate placement of these amulets suggests a purposeful act, demonstrating a conscious effort to utilize the cat's power to facilitate a safe passage for the soul.

The textual evidence, although less explicit, indirectly reinforces this concept. While there isn't a direct declaration proclaiming cats as afterlife guides, the rich mythology surrounding feline deities provides compelling circumstantial evidence. Bastet, the most prominent cat goddess, is inextricably linked to both protection and the home, and her association with childbirth extends her influence into the cycle of life and death, suggesting a natural transition into her role as a protector of souls. The very act of mummifying a cat, mirroring the processes applied to humans, signifies a belief in the continued existence of the feline's spirit. The elaborate preparation and inclusion of grave goods, especially those suggesting comfort and sustenance, further highlight the expectation of the cat's continued existence alongside the deceased. This isn't simply disposal of a pet; this is preparing a companion for a journey.

The association of cats with other deities associated with the afterlife, such as Sekhmet and Mafdet, adds further layers to this interpretation. Sekhmet, the lion-headed goddess of war and disease, is often viewed as a powerful protector, capable of vanquishing threats. Her presence, even in a fierce form, suggests the cat's role in protecting the deceased from the dangers of the underworld. Mafdet, the cat-goddess of justice, implies a role in ensuring a fair passage through the judgment process, guiding the soul towards its rightful destination. The diverse depictions of these goddesses, and their association with feline forms, suggests a versatile spiritual function for cats in the afterlife, able to provide both protection and guidance throughout the complex processes of death and judgment.

It's important to note that the notion of cats as afterlife guides wasn't universally applied. The degree of care and extravagance bestowed upon the mummified cats varied considerably,

reflecting social status and possibly the perceived significance of the individual feline. A cherished pet from a wealthy household might have received a far more elaborate burial than a working cat, suggesting a variable degree of belief in the cat's afterlife influence based on its perceived earthly importance. However, the very fact that even less elaborate cat burials existed speaks to the widespread belief that these animals held some spiritual significance, even if their roles within the afterlife were not equally weighted.

The diversity in the artistic representations of cats within funerary contexts further underscores this point. While some depictions clearly show cats accompanying the deceased, others may present them as symbolic representations of deities or as simply a part of the deceased's earthly possessions that continued to accompany them. This variance highlights the complex nature of ancient Egyptian beliefs; the role of cats in the afterlife was nuanced and multifaceted, encompassing both personal and religious significance. The study of individual burials, therefore, requires a careful consideration of the context and the specific iconography used to fully appreciate the role of a specific feline within the deceased's afterlife journey.

Furthermore, the scientific analysis of cat mummies contributes crucial evidence to this ongoing discussion. Studies of their diet, age, and overall health provide insights into their lifestyles and their relationships with humans, enhancing our understanding of their role in society and their potential spiritual significance. The fact that considerable resources were devoted to their mummification, often mirroring the care given to human mummies, highlights the significant value placed on these creatures, even in death. This dedication suggests more than mere sentimentality; it strongly indicates a belief in their continued existence and participation in the afterlife.

The study of ancient Egyptian beliefs about the afterlife consistently reveals a complex system of interactions between the living, the dead, and the divine. The integration of cats into this intricate system, evidenced by the overwhelming archaeological evidence and artistic representations, strongly suggests a belief in their role as guides or protectors. Their ability to navigate both the physical and spiritual realms, symbolized by their agility and nocturnal habits, placed them in a unique position to assist the deceased in their transition to the Duat. The meticulous preparation and often extravagant burials of cats stand as testament to this profound and enduring belief in the feline's power to mediate the passage between life and death. The continued research into feline burials remains crucial in unlocking a deeper understanding of this fascinating interaction between humans, animals, and the spiritual world of ancient Egypt.

The comprehensive examination of these practices, ranging from detailed analysis of grave goods to the scientific analysis of the mummified remains, continues to provide valuable insight into the religious beliefs, social structures, and emotional lives of the ancient Egyptians. The more we learn about these rituals, the richer our understanding of this remarkable civilization becomes. The enduring legacy of these beliefs, interwoven with the lives of both humans and their beloved feline companions, continues to captivate and inspire wonder in the present day. The mystery, however, remains partially veiled, inviting further investigation and further illuminating the complex and enduring relationship between ancient Egyptians and their revered cats. The meticulous study of cat mummies, therefore, offers a unique and invaluable lens through which to further examine and understand the intricate tapestry of ancient Egyptian beliefs surrounding death, the afterlife, and the profound connection between humans and animals.

The Significance of Cat Burials

The sheer scale of cat burials in ancient Egypt presents a compelling argument for the profound societal impact of this practice, extending far beyond individual piety or simple pet devotion. The economic implications alone are staggering. Mummification, even for a relatively small animal, required skilled labor, specific materials such as linen bandages and resins, and dedicated spaces for the process. The resources devoted to the mummification of countless cats represent a significant investment of time, effort, and resources, a testament to the societal value placed upon these animals. Consider the cost of the embalming process itself: the acquisition of natron, the essential desiccant, the careful removal of internal organs, the application of resins and oils for preservation, and finally, the wrapping and placement of the mummified cat within its sarcophagus or burial shroud. This was not a casual undertaking; it was a complex ritual requiring specialized knowledge and considerable expense. The scale of these operations, particularly when considering the numerous large cat cemeteries discovered throughout Egypt, underscores the immense economic impact of this religious practice.

Beyond the purely economic considerations, the widespread practice of cat mummification reveals a complex interplay between religious institutions, societal norms, and economic realities. The existence of large-scale cat cemeteries, such as the one discovered at Beni Hasan, suggests a highly organized and centralized system for handling the disposal of deceased cats. These cemeteries were not haphazard collections of discarded animals; they were carefully planned and managed sites, often requiring significant land allocation and ongoing maintenance. The implications are far-reaching. The very existence of these sites indicates the level of societal acceptance and even encouragement of cat mummification, supported by the resources and labor required to manage such an undertaking. It suggests a level of social organization and religious infrastructure capable of supporting a large-scale funerary operation dedicated specifically to cats.

The social organization involved in the cat mummification process is equally fascinating. While much of the labor was likely carried out by skilled professionals within temples or dedicated funerary establishments, the participation of wider society is undeniable. The sheer number of cats mummified necessitates the involvement of many individuals, not only for the mummification itself but also for the collection, transportation, and preparation of the bodies. This widespread participation implies a level of community involvement in the religious practice, highlighting the shared beliefs and cultural norms that sustained this unique custom. It transcends a simple elite-driven practice; the widespread nature of cat mummification suggests that individuals across various social strata actively participated in, or at least condoned, this ritual.

Further complicating the issue is the evident variation in the quality and extravagance of cat burials. While some cats received elaborate mummification and burial rites, complete with sarcophagi and grave goods, others were treated with far less ceremony. This variation likely reflects social status, with wealthy individuals potentially affording more lavish treatment for their beloved pets, while those of lower social standing may have offered more modest burials. However, the very fact that even simpler burials existed is significant; it demonstrates the broad societal acceptance of the practice, and the inherent value attributed to the cat itself, irrespective of the resources invested in its burial. This variation in funerary practices highlights the complex interplay between social status, religious belief, and economic capability within ancient Egyptian society.

The societal impact also extended to the role of religious institutions. Temples dedicated to feline deities, such as Bastet, likely played a significant role in organizing and managing the cat mummification process. These institutions may have provided the necessary facilities, trained personnel, and religious guidance for the proper performance of the rites. The economic prosperity of these temples may have been, in part, dependent on the offerings and donations related to cat burials. Furthermore, the widespread reverence for cats and the elaborate nature

of their burials likely reinforced the authority and influence of the priestly classes, further consolidating the link between religious institutions and societal norms.

The discovery of vast cat cemeteries provides concrete evidence for the scale of this practice. These sites often contained thousands, even tens of thousands of mummified cats, indicating an immense and sustained effort to honor these creatures in death. The sheer volume of these discoveries is astonishing, emphasizing the societal commitment to this funerary custom. Moreover, these cemeteries are not just repositories of deceased cats; they represent a significant investment of land, labor, and resources, reflecting the immense cultural and religious significance of cats within ancient Egyptian society. Analysis of these sites reveals not only the sheer scale of the practice, but also provides valuable insights into the organizational methods, economic infrastructure, and social structure that supported it.

In summary, the analysis of cat burials reveals much more than mere animal devotion. The practice represents a complex interaction between religious beliefs, societal norms, and economic realities. The scale of cat mummification, the existence of large-scale cemeteries, and the variation in burial practices all contribute to a multifaceted understanding of the profound influence cats had on ancient Egyptian society. The economic impact was considerable, requiring significant resources and labor. The social implications were extensive, involving the participation of a wide range of individuals and demonstrating the deep-seated societal acceptance of the practice. And finally, the religious implications were equally significant, reinforcing the authority of temples and priests and reflecting the profound spiritual significance attributed to cats.

The legacy of these beliefs and practices continues to resonate today, reminding us of the remarkable and enduring relationship between ancient Egyptians and their revered feline companions. The detailed study of these cemeteries, combined with scientific analysis of mummified remains, holds the key to unlocking a much more nuanced understanding of ancient Egyptian religious practices and the role of animals within their complex and fascinating society.

Cats in Ancient Egyptian Medicine

Chapter Five

The reverence afforded to cats in ancient Egypt extended beyond funerary rituals and religious iconography; hints emerge suggesting a possible, albeit poorly documented, role for felines in ancient Egyptian medicine. While no explicit texts detail the widespread use of cats in medicinal preparations akin to the use of other animals, the pervasive association of cats with healing deities and their symbolic links to regeneration and vitality warrant investigation. The absence of clear evidence, however, shouldn't be interpreted as conclusive proof of their absence from medicinal practices. The limited surviving medical papyri primarily focus on herbal remedies, surgical techniques, and diagnostic methods, offering a somewhat incomplete picture of the full spectrum of ancient Egyptian healthcare.

One crucial aspect to consider is the difficulty in definitively separating religious beliefs from medical practices in ancient Egypt. The lines often blurred, with healing frequently attributed to divine intervention or magical forces. Many deities, including Sekhmet, a lion-headed goddess associated with healing and disease, possessed feline attributes, suggesting a potential connection between feline symbolism and the healing arts. The association of Bastet, the cat goddess, with protection and fertility, might also imply a tangential link to health and well-being, though direct evidence is lacking. Interpreting this symbolic connection requires careful consideration, as it's tempting to draw conclusions based on religious imagery without concrete supporting evidence.

The Ebers Papyrus, one of the most important surviving medical texts, offers a comprehensive overview of ancient Egyptian medical knowledge. While it details numerous herbal remedies, surgical techniques, and diagnostic methods, it makes no direct mention of cats in medicinal contexts. This silence is significant, but it does not definitively exclude the possibility of cats being used in localized or less documented practices. The Ebers Papyrus, while extensive, may not represent the entirety of Egyptian medical knowledge, potentially omitting less common or regionally specific practices.

Similarly, the Edwin Smith Papyrus, focusing on surgical techniques, contains no reference to cats. The text demonstrates a surprisingly advanced understanding of anatomy and surgical procedures for various injuries. Yet, its silence regarding the use of cats in healing does not entirely discount the possibility of their limited application. The selective nature of surviving texts hampers a complete picture of ancient Egyptian medical practices, and the lack of mention might simply reflect the limitations of our currently accessible sources.

Another avenue of inquiry is the potential use of cat-related products in medicinal preparations. While the Ebers Papyrus doesn't explicitly detail the use of cat parts, it extensively documents the use of a vast array of animal products in various remedies. This raises the possibility that cat-derived substances, such as fat, bone, or even fur, might have found limited use in some medicinal practices. However, without direct textual evidence, any assertion remains speculative. The careful examination of mummified animal remains from medical contexts could potentially yield further insights into this area, although contamination and the challenges of definitively identifying materials thousands of years old present considerable obstacles.

The possibility of cat fat being used as an ointment or balm is an intriguing consideration. Animal fats were commonly used in ancient Egyptian medicine for their emollient properties, and cat fat might have been deemed suitable for certain ailments. This hypothesis, however,

remains entirely speculative, requiring further research and perhaps the discovery of relevant archaeological evidence to support it. Similarly, certain cat bones could have been considered suitable for creating amulets or charms to provide protection against illness or injury. Such practices, however, would fall more into the realm of magical medicine and would need careful distinction from direct medicinal application.

Furthermore, the cat's association with certain deities might have led to the belief in its inherent healing properties. The connection between the feline and the realm of the divine could have influenced the perceptions of the cat's medicinal potential. Individuals might have attributed healing to divine intercession mediated through the presence of a cat, or through the use of objects associated with the feline deity. Such beliefs, while difficult to empirically verify, undoubtedly played a significant role in shaping the healthcare practices of ancient Egypt. We must therefore consider the complex interaction between religious beliefs, cultural norms, and practical medical practices.

The lack of explicit textual evidence regarding the medicinal use of cats should be considered in context. The surviving medical papyri represent only a fragment of ancient Egyptian medical knowledge. Many practices may have been transmitted orally, lost to time, or simply not recorded in the surviving texts. The potential use of cats in medicine might have been a localized or less formalized practice, not considered significant enough to warrant inclusion in the more formal and canonical medical texts.

The absence of explicit evidence, however, does not completely negate the possibility of cats playing a minor or localized role in ancient Egyptian medical practices. Further research, including the analysis of archaeological remains and a more comprehensive study of surviving texts, could potentially reveal more evidence. Moreover, a more nuanced understanding of the complex interplay between religious belief and medical practice in ancient Egypt is necessary to fully appreciate the potential role of cats within their healing traditions. The symbolic power of the cat, combined with the common use of animal parts in Egyptian medicine, leaves open the intriguing possibility of limited or localized use of feline-related components in ancient Egyptian healing practices. Until further evidence emerges, however, this remains a fascinating but ultimately speculative area of study. The potential remains, however, a compelling area of ongoing research within the intricate tapestry of ancient Egyptian culture and belief. The exploration of the relationship between cats, deities and healing demands a further deeper analysis of the broader religious and cultural context, for it provides a glimpse into the multifaceted nature of ancient Egyptian medical thinking and practices, highlighting the importance of considering factors beyond the purely scientific and practical.

Magical Properties Attributed to Cats

The pervasive reverence for cats in ancient Egypt extended far beyond their religious and potential medicinal roles; they were deeply interwoven into the fabric of ancient Egyptian magic. The feline form, embodying grace, agility, and a perceived connection to the unseen, became a potent symbol in amulets, spells, and magical rituals. These practices reveal a profound belief in the cat's inherent magical capabilities, extending their influence from the earthly realm to the spiritual plane.

One of the most compelling pieces of evidence for the magical properties attributed to cats lies in the abundance of feline-shaped amulets unearthed from ancient Egyptian tombs and settlements. These amulets, crafted from various materials such as faience, carnelian, and precious metals, often depict cats in a variety of postures and contexts. Some depict Bastet, the lion-headed goddess, in her benevolent form, while others simply feature stylized feline figures, suggesting a broader association of the cat form with protective magic. The sheer number of these amulets, discovered across various periods of ancient Egyptian history, underscores the widespread belief in their magical efficacy.

The purpose of these amulets often extended beyond simple religious devotion. Many were clearly intended to serve as protective charms, safeguarding the wearer from illness, injury, or misfortune. The placement of these amulets, often found nestled against the body or within funerary wrappings, further reinforces this protective function. Scholars believe the amulets were believed to channel the protective power of the feline deity, Bastet, warding off evil spirits and ensuring the well-being of the wearer. The diversity in size and materials used suggests a range of amulets designed for various needs and purposes, catering to different social classes and individual preferences.

Beyond the protective amulets, feline imagery appears in a range of other magical contexts. Ancient Egyptian spells and incantations frequently invoke the power of feline deities, particularly Bastet, seeking their protection and intervention in various aspects of life. These magical texts, preserved in papyri and tomb inscriptions, reveal a complex system of beliefs and rituals where cats served as intermediaries between the human and divine realms. The invocation of Bastet in these spells showcases her significant role as a protective deity, capable of influencing events and outcomes in the earthly realm.

The careful study of these spells reveals a detailed understanding of the ritualistic practices associated with feline magic. These practices varied depending on the specific objective, ranging from ensuring protection during childbirth to warding off evil spirits and seeking divine intervention during times of illness or misfortune. The inclusion of feline imagery and the invocation of feline deities in these rituals highlights the central role cats played in ancient Egyptian magical practices, acting as conduits of divine power and intermediaries within the spiritual realm. The detailed descriptions of these rituals offer valuable insights into the beliefs and practices of ancient Egyptian magic, revealing a sophisticated system deeply intertwined with the veneration of feline deities.

The use of cat-related materials in magical practices further reinforces the perceived magical potency of the feline. While the direct use of cat parts in spells remains a point of scholarly debate, the use of materials associated with cats, such as cat fur, bone, or claws, in amulets and other magical objects is well documented. These materials were believed to possess the residual magical energy of the feline, imbuing the magical objects with protective and healing properties. The crafting of these amulets and objects was likely a specialized practice, requiring specific knowledge and skills to harness the magical power of the feline.

The inclusion of cat imagery in tomb paintings and funerary texts further underscores the magical significance attributed to cats. These depictions, often portraying cats alongside other protective deities or symbolic imagery, suggest a connection between feline magic and the

afterlife. The belief that cats could provide protection and guidance in the journey to the afterlife reinforces their significant role in both earthly and spiritual realms. The continued presence of feline imagery in funerary contexts across centuries illustrates the enduring belief in the cat's power to protect and guide the deceased.

The precise nature of the magical properties attributed to cats remains a complex and fascinating area of research. While the surviving texts and artifacts offer glimpses into ancient Egyptian beliefs and practices, the limitations of available evidence prevent a complete understanding of the nuances of their magical worldview. However, the pervasive presence of feline imagery in amulets, spells, and funerary contexts provides undeniable evidence of the significant role cats played in ancient Egyptian magic, highlighting their perceived connection to the spiritual realm and their power to influence events in both earthly and spiritual realms.

The connection between cats and the sun god Ra also adds another layer to the magical perception of cats. Some scholars suggest that the cat's association with the sun's power amplified their significance in protective magic. The cat's ability to see in low light might have also contributed to the association with the nocturnal world, hinting at a connection to other mystical forces. This duality, the association with both solar and nocturnal forces, enhanced the mystical attributes of the cat. This dual nature, capable of both protecting from the sun's glare and seeing in the darkness, made the cat a powerful symbolic guardian.

It is important to note that the magical practices involving cats weren't always simple or straightforward. The effectiveness of the magic was believed to depend on factors such as the timing, the specific rituals performed, and the intention of the practitioner. This element of ritualistic precision in the utilization of cat-related magic emphasizes the meticulousness and careful consideration that the ancient Egyptians placed upon their magical practices. The process was not simply about possessing an amulet but also understanding and correctly performing the associated rituals to engage the cat's supposed magical power.

Moreover, the interpretation of feline symbolism varied depending on the cultural and religious context. While Bastet represented the benevolent and protective aspects of the feline, other feline deities, like Sekhmet, possessed more fierce and powerful attributes, reflecting the varied perceptions of the feline's magical capabilities. This diversity in feline representation further underscores the complex interplay between religious belief, cultural norms, and magical practices in ancient Egypt. The nuance in the utilization of cat-based magic reflects the sophisticated understanding of spiritual forces in ancient Egyptian society.

The study of feline magic in ancient Egypt also requires consideration of the wider context of ancient Egyptian magic. Cats were not isolated figures within this broader system but were integrated into a complex web of magical beliefs and practices involving various deities, rituals, and amulets. Understanding the cat's role requires a comprehensive analysis of this broader system, avoiding simplistic interpretations of their magical significance. The integration of feline magic within the larger framework of ancient Egyptian magical beliefs offers a more complete understanding of their culture and worldview.

Finally, the enduring legacy of the magical properties attributed to cats in ancient Egypt continues to resonate even today. The enduring popularity of cat-themed amulets and the continued fascination with ancient Egyptian magic serve as a testament to the enduring power of the feline in the collective imagination. The study of ancient Egyptian magic offers a glimpse into a unique and complex culture, enriching our understanding of the human relationship with the natural world and the spiritual realm. The enduring appeal of cat-related magic highlights the powerful symbolism of the feline and its enduring connection to the mysteries of ancient Egypt. The investigation into the magical properties attributed to cats in ancient Egypt provides a rich tapestry of insights into the religious, cultural, and magical beliefs of this remarkable civilization.

Cats and the Practice of Witchcraft

The preceding discussion established the overwhelmingly positive and protective association of cats, particularly through their connection to Bastet, within ancient Egyptian magic and religious practices. However, the nuanced and complex nature of ancient Egyptian beliefs necessitates a further examination into whether any evidence suggests a darker, more ambivalent, or even negative perception of cats existed within specific contexts, potentially touching upon themes associated with what we might understand as "witchcraft." Such an exploration must be undertaken cautiously, avoiding anachronistic interpretations imposed upon ancient beliefs.

The absence of direct, explicit condemnation of cats as inherently "evil" or associated with malevolent magic in readily available primary sources is striking. The vast majority of evidence points towards their overwhelmingly positive symbolic value. Yet, the complexities of ancient Egyptian religion and magic defy simplistic categorization. The possibility of negative connotations associated with cats in specific circumstances, perhaps even within certain magical practices, warrants closer scrutiny. This examination must focus not on an inherent "evil" in the cat itself but rather on a potential contextual shift in its symbolic meaning.

One avenue for exploring this nuanced perspective involves examining the symbolism of other feline deities beyond Bastet. While Bastet embodied benevolent protection, Sekhmet, the lion-headed goddess of war and disease, represented a powerful, potentially destructive, aspect of the feline form. Sekhmet's role in inflicting punishment and disease, while serving a wider cosmic purpose, introduces an element of fear and the potential for harm associated with feline power. However, even in Sekhmet's case, the fear is not directed at the feline form itself, but rather the divine power she embodies. The cat remains a powerful symbol, albeit one associated with destruction rather than protection. Her iconography often includes a powerful roar, suggesting a more aggressive and less approachable deity than the gentle

Bastet. This duality within the feline goddesses reveals a spectrum of potential associations, shifting the symbolism away from a solely benevolent perspective.

Another area of investigation involves analyzing the potential role of cats in funerary rituals. While cats were often mummified and buried with elaborate care, reflecting their revered status, the absence of cats in certain contexts might be significant. This absence could indicate selective inclusion based on beliefs about the afterlife or specific funerary practices. The absence of feline imagery in some tombs, for instance, might not represent a negative connotation, but a conscious choice reflecting the beliefs of the deceased or the family. Further investigation could also determine if any specific types of cats, such as black cats, were treated differently or held different symbolic meanings. It is crucial to avoid imposing modern superstitions on ancient beliefs.

Furthermore, the interpretation of spells and incantations requires careful consideration. While many spells invoked the protective power of Bastet, others may have utilized feline imagery in more complex or ambiguous ways. The context of the spell, the accompanying rituals, and the overall intention of the practitioner are crucial for understanding the role of the feline symbol. An isolated instance of feline imagery in a negative context should not be interpreted as a widespread condemnation but rather analyzed within the larger framework of the spell's purpose and the beliefs of its user. The subtleties of the ancient Egyptian language and the limited nature of surviving texts often necessitate careful and nuanced interpretation to avoid misrepresenting the intended meaning.

The use of materials derived from cats in magical practices also requires careful consideration. While the use of cat-related items in amulets is widely documented, the specific circumstances of their use warrant further investigation. It is crucial to avoid assuming a simple correlation between the use of cat-derived materials and malevolent magic. The meaning and effectiveness

of the magical practice depend significantly on the rituals, the intentions of the practitioner, and the overall context of the spell or ritual. Again, the lack of clear evidence supporting the use of cat parts in spells designed to cause harm stands in stark contrast to the overwhelmingly protective associations found in the broader corpus of ancient Egyptian magical practices.

To further refine the investigation, it is helpful to compare and contrast the treatment of cats with the treatment of other animals in ancient Egypt. Did the Egyptians attribute magical or spiritual properties to other animals, and if so, how did these compare with the beliefs surrounding cats? Exploring parallels and contrasts within the broader context of ancient Egyptian animistic beliefs and their treatment of different animals may shed light on the particular significance accorded to cats.

The limited surviving evidence prevents a definitive conclusion about the existence of negative connotations associated with cats in ancient Egyptian witchcraft. The overwhelming evidence points towards a strong positive association with protection and divine power. However, the nuances within the feline deities themselves, the possibilities of varied interpretations within funerary practices, and the complexities of spell interpretations all suggest the need for a multi-faceted approach to avoid oversimplification. The picture is far more complex than a simple dichotomy of good and evil. The potential for a darker, more ambivalent perspective on cats in certain specific magical practices warrants further investigation; however, no concrete evidence currently supports the idea of widespread negative association with cats as inherently linked to witchcraft or malevolent magic. The primary sources consistently highlight the overwhelmingly positive and protective role of cats within ancient Egyptian society's magical and religious world. The study continues to offer a fascinating glimpse into the intricate and multifaceted beliefs of a remarkable civilization.

Cat Related Spells and Incantations

The pervasive positive association of cats with protection and divine power in ancient Egypt, primarily through their link to the goddess Bastet, is undeniable. However, a complete understanding of the feline's role in ancient Egyptian magic necessitates a deeper exploration of spells and incantations specifically involving cats. These spells, preserved on papyri, inscribed on amulets, and alluded to in other textual fragments, offer valuable insights into the beliefs and practices surrounding feline magic. The analysis must avoid imposing modern interpretations onto ancient practices, focusing instead on understanding the context and intent within the ancient Egyptian worldview.

One crucial aspect of this investigation involves analyzing the language employed in these spells. The ancient Egyptian language, with its nuances and subtleties, often requires careful consideration of word choice and grammatical structure to discern the true meaning. For example, the use of specific verbs and adjectives in relation to cats may indicate different levels of power, protection, or even potential harm, depending on the overall context. The lack of standardized translation across different scholarly works often necessitates a comparative approach, allowing for a more nuanced understanding.

Furthermore, the material components of the spells themselves provide important clues. The use of cat-related materials, such as cat fur, claws, or bones, in amulets and magical preparations, is well documented. However, interpreting the significance of these materials requires careful analysis. Simply finding a cat's claw in an amulet does not automatically indicate a negative intent. The amulet's overall design, the other materials included, and the accompanying rituals all contribute to its interpretation.

Several spells specifically mention Bastet's protective power. These spells often invoke Bastet's name and attribute to her the ability to ward off evil spirits, protect against disease, and ensure fertility and prosperity. The language used typically employs respectful and reverential terms, reinforcing Bastet's benevolent nature and the Egyptians' faith in her protective power. For example, spells requesting protection for childbirth often feature Bastet prominently, emphasizing her nurturing and life-giving aspects. These spells would often involve ritualistic practices alongside the incantations, such as burning incense, making offerings, or carrying a specific amulet.

Interestingly, some spells, while not explicitly negative, employ feline imagery in more ambivalent or complex ways. For example, certain spells for healing might utilize imagery relating to the predatory aspects of cats. This does not imply a negative connotation; rather, it suggests the invocation of the cat's powerful and forceful nature to overcome illness. It is similar to the symbolism of Sekhmet, where the lion-headed goddess, while capable of inflicting disease, is also a powerful healer. This duality highlights the complex relationship between cats and the concept of power within ancient Egyptian magical beliefs. The cat's power is not inherently good or evil, but rather a force that can be channeled for various purposes depending on the practitioner's intent and the context of the ritual.

Analysis of spells relating to protection against malicious magic or supernatural threats also provides insightful information. The use of cat imagery in these contexts strongly emphasizes Bastet's protective ability. The spells often depict Bastet confronting and vanquishing evil spirits or hostile magical forces. These descriptions further reinforce the strong positive association between cats and protection from harm. However, the existence of these protective spells implicitly acknowledges the belief in malevolent forces, showcasing a complex worldview which acknowledged both positive and negative forces existing simultaneously within the cosmos.

The limited number of surviving spells focusing on potentially negative contexts requires cautious interpretation. While some scholars have suggested the potential for feline imagery in spells associated with negative magical effects, the absence of definitive evidence and the overwhelming evidence of positive associations necessitate careful consideration. Any interpretation must be supported by strong textual evidence and placed firmly within the larger context of ancient Egyptian beliefs and practices. Simply finding feline imagery in a spell associated with misfortune does not automatically equate cats with causing that misfortune.

Another important aspect for research is the potential geographical and temporal variations in beliefs surrounding cat magic. Different regions of ancient Egypt may have had subtly different beliefs and practices, and these variations might be reflected in the spells and incantations discovered in those areas. Similarly, changes in beliefs and practices over time could also lead to subtle shifts in how cats were viewed and incorporated into magical rituals. Therefore, a thorough examination would require geographical and chronological classification of all available sources to identify and analyze these potentially significant variations.

Comparing and contrasting spells involving cats with spells employing other animals within the ancient Egyptian pantheon further enriches our understanding. Consider the use of other animals in protection spells. Were these other animals seen as having comparable power to cats, or did cats possess a uniquely significant role in protection? This comparative analysis could illuminate the specific reasons behind the extraordinary reverence shown towards cats. The comparison should move beyond simple similarities and explore the underlying symbolic structures and their significance within the ancient worldview. Were these symbols interchangeable, or did each possess specific attributes that made them suitable for different magical applications?

The study of ancient Egyptian spells related to cats offers a rich and complex tapestry of magical beliefs and practices. While the evidence strongly points towards an overwhelmingly positive and protective association between cats and magic, the subtle nuances within the language, the material components of the spells, and the varied contexts of their use require careful and nuanced analysis. The absence of significant evidence pointing to a widespread negative association underscores the cat's revered status. However, the continued study and comparative analysis of extant spells and related artifacts are crucial for uncovering the complete picture of the feline's multifaceted role in the fascinating world of ancient Egyptian magic. The research continues to yield valuable insights into the intricate and profoundly significant place of the cat within ancient Egyptian religion and culture. Further investigation might explore the transmission of these beliefs and practices, considering the potential influence of Egyptian magic on other cultures and the enduring legacy of the cat's sacred status. The enigma remains a captivating subject for scholarly pursuit.

The Legacy of Feline Magic

The enduring legacy of feline magic in ancient Egypt extends far beyond the confines of the pharaonic era. Its influence can be traced through the centuries, subtly shaping magical practices and beliefs in various cultures that came into contact with Egyptian civilization, both directly and indirectly. The association of cats with magic, mystery, and the supernatural, so deeply ingrained in ancient Egyptian thought, found fertile ground for propagation and adaptation in new environments.

The spread of Egyptian religious beliefs, including those surrounding feline deities like Bastet, played a crucial role in this transmission. The conquest of Egypt by various empires, such as the Greeks, Romans, and later the Byzantines, resulted in the dissemination of Egyptian religious iconography and mythology throughout the Mediterranean world. While the dominant religions of these empires largely supplanted the Egyptian pantheon, elements of Egyptian magical beliefs, including the veneration of cats, persisted, often undergoing syncretism with local traditions. We see evidence of this in Roman-era amulets featuring feline imagery alongside Roman deities, hinting at the adoption and adaptation of Egyptian beliefs into a new cultural context.

The persistence of Egyptian magical papyri also played a significant role. These texts, containing spells and incantations, were sometimes preserved and copied, even long after the decline of the pharaonic era. While many of these papyri were likely intended for practical use – such as healing or protection – the inclusion of feline symbolism or references to Bastet's power would have served to reinforce the cat's already existing association with magic in the minds of those who consulted them. The continued study and use of these texts by later practitioners of magic and divination likely contributed to the perpetuation of feline-related magical beliefs.

The transmission of these beliefs was not always direct. Sometimes, it involved a more subtle process of cultural exchange and adaptation. For example, the symbolic association of cats with independence, agility, and nocturnal activity—attributes already recognized in ancient Egypt—may have independently reinforced their association with witchcraft and magic in later European folk traditions. The notion of cats as familiars, common in medieval and Renaissance witchcraft lore, echoes the ancient Egyptian concept of cats as powerful intermediaries between the human and divine worlds. This suggests a parallel development based on similar, if not directly inherited, symbolic interpretations.

The role of trade networks should also be considered in understanding the dissemination of feline-related beliefs. The exchange of goods and ideas across the Mediterranean, and even further afield, facilitated the movement of cultural motifs and religious symbols. The presence of Egyptian-style amulets and artifacts in distant locations points to a wider dissemination of beliefs and practices than previously thought. This exchange wasn't merely a one-way street; rather, the interaction between different cultures often resulted in the blending of traditions and the adaptation of existing beliefs to suit new contexts.

The specific ways in which Egyptian beliefs about feline magic were adapted varied considerably depending on the receiving culture. In some cases, the veneration of Bastet was directly incorporated into local pantheons. In others, the feline imagery was adapted, and the associated beliefs were reinterpreted to fit into pre-existing systems of magic and divination. This process of syncretism demonstrates the remarkable adaptability of these beliefs and their ability to survive and transform within new cultural landscapes.

Furthermore, the continued presence of cats in human societies across various cultures suggests that the intuitive sense of the cat's unique qualities – independence, intelligence, and a seeming connection to the unseen world—played a role in maintaining its association with

the magical or mystical. The very qualities that led to their veneration in ancient Egypt likely continued to resonate with people across different eras and geographical locations.

The influence of ancient Egyptian beliefs about feline magic can even be traced into more modern occult traditions. The enduring fascination with cats in various esoteric systems, from Wicca to various forms of modern paganism, showcases the continued resonance of these ancient beliefs. Though the specific practices and beliefs may have changed over time, the underlying association of cats with magic and mystery remains a powerful and persistent element.

It's important to avoid romanticizing or exaggerating the direct influence of ancient Egyptian beliefs. The transmission of cultural elements is a complex process, often involving multiple layers of influence, adaptation, and transformation. While we can trace clear connections between ancient Egyptian beliefs and later traditions, it's crucial to recognize the unique features and developments within these later traditions as well.

A comprehensive understanding of the legacy of feline magic requires a comparative approach, acknowledging the interplay between various cultural influences. It demands careful study of the historical and archaeological record, including the analysis of artifacts, texts, and iconography from different periods and cultures. This multi-faceted approach is crucial for unraveling the intricate web of connections and influences that shaped the enduring association of cats with magic and the supernatural. The enduring presence of feline magic in the tapestry of world culture is a testament to the power of ancient Egyptian beliefs and the enduring fascination with the enigmatic nature of the cat.

The study of feline magic in ancient Egypt and its legacy is not merely an academic exercise; it sheds light on the enduring human fascination with animals and the supernatural. It underscores the remarkable capacity of cultural beliefs to transcend geographical and temporal boundaries, adapting and transforming as they journey through time and across cultures. The continuing association of cats with magic and the unseen remains a compelling testament to the power of ancient beliefs and the enduring allure of the feline world. This persistent connection highlights the intricate and multifaceted nature of human-animal relationships, demonstrating the deep-seated symbolic and spiritual significance that animals, particularly cats, have held throughout history. The study of this enduring legacy offers insights not only into ancient Egyptian culture but also into the universal human tendency to find meaning and magic in the natural world, particularly in creatures that hold a unique place in our hearts and minds.

The ongoing research into the dissemination and transformation of ancient Egyptian beliefs about feline magic promises to uncover even more fascinating connections and shed further light on the rich tapestry of cultural exchange and the enduring power of ancient traditions. As we continue to explore the legacy of this ancient reverence, we gain a deeper appreciation for the enduring fascination with the mysterious and magical attributes long associated with cats, a fascination that spans millennia and continues to shape our understanding of the world. The whispers of Bastet, once confined to the temples and tombs of ancient Egypt, continue to echo in the mystical traditions of the world, reminding us of the enduring power of ancient beliefs and the enduring mystique of the feline form.

The Decline of Cat Worship in Egypt

Chapter Six

The unwavering reverence for cats in ancient Egypt, a devotion that spanned millennia, did not endure indefinitely. The gradual decline of widespread cat worship, a process unfolding over centuries, was a complex phenomenon interwoven with broader societal and religious transformations within Egypt itself and the influences of conquering powers. While the complete eradication of feline veneration never truly occurred—residual beliefs and practices persisted in various forms—the formerly pervasive and deeply ingrained societal acceptance of cats as sacred beings gradually faded.

One significant factor contributing to the decline was the gradual erosion of the ancient Egyptian religious system itself. The rise and spread of Christianity, beginning in the late Roman period, presented a formidable challenge to the traditional polytheistic beliefs. Christianity, with its monotheistic emphasis and its condemnation of idolatry, was fundamentally at odds with the Egyptian pantheon, which included numerous gods and goddesses, and their animal manifestations, such as Bastet. The conversion of the Egyptian population to Christianity, a process that unfolded over centuries, inevitably led to a diminished role for feline deities within the religious landscape. Temples dedicated to Bastet and other feline deities were abandoned, their once-sacred spaces eventually falling into ruin or being repurposed for other uses.

The Roman conquest of Egypt in 30 BC marked a pivotal turning point. While the Romans initially adopted a policy of religious tolerance, allowing the continued practice of traditional Egyptian beliefs, this tolerance gradually waned. The Roman emphasis on their own pantheon of gods, alongside the growing influence of Christianity, exerted increasing pressure on the traditional Egyptian religious system. The official patronage and support enjoyed by Egyptian deities during the pharaonic era ceased, and the resources dedicated to their worship dwindled. This diminished patronage directly impacted the scale and frequency of religious festivals and ceremonies honoring cats and their associated deities. The grand celebrations and processions that once characterized the worship of Bastet became less common, eventually ceasing altogether in many areas.

Furthermore, the Roman administration, in its efforts to consolidate its control and suppress potential unrest, may have actively discouraged practices perceived as overtly pagan or potentially subversive. While there's no direct evidence of systematic persecution of cat worship, the Roman authorities may have subtly discouraged certain aspects of the religion, particularly those that involved extensive public displays of devotion or deviated from the prevailing norms of Roman society. This subtle pressure, combined with the broader religious shifts, likely contributed to the decline in the prominence of cat worship.

Beyond the direct influence of Christianity and Roman rule, several other factors contributed to the fading reverence for cats. The gradual decline of literacy in ancient Egypt, following the end of the pharaonic era, hindered the transmission of knowledge about traditional religious beliefs and practices. The loss of written records, including religious texts and magical papyri relating to feline deities, meant that the detailed knowledge and rituals surrounding cat worship became less accessible to succeeding generations. This loss of knowledge, combined with the spread of new religious and cultural influences, gradually eroded the understanding and appreciation of the nuanced beliefs once central to feline veneration.

The economic and political instability that characterized much of the late Roman and Byzantine periods also played a role. The widespread social upheaval, coupled with declining,

Economic prosperity, may have diverted attention and resources away from religious practices, including the worship of cats. In times of hardship and uncertainty, people may have been more inclined to focus on matters of immediate survival rather than elaborate religious observances. This pragmatic shift in priorities likely contributed to the diminished importance of cat worship within the broader societal context.

However, it's crucial to understand that the decline of cat worship was not a sudden or complete event. Instead, it was a gradual process spanning several centuries, marked by a diminishing societal emphasis on feline veneration rather than outright suppression or eradication. While grand temples and large-scale public rituals dedicated to Bastet and other feline deities eventually disappeared, many individual Egyptians likely continued to hold personal beliefs and practice private rituals associated with cats. The feline remained a cherished companion animal, and many individuals may have continued to revere the cat for its perceived supernatural attributes, albeit within a changing religious and cultural framework.

Evidence suggests that even after the decline of prominent cat worship, certain aspects of feline-related beliefs and practices persisted. These surviving elements often intertwined with emerging religious traditions, creating syncretic forms of worship. In some instances, aspects of Bastet's character or attributes might have been assimilated into new religious figures or concepts. Similarly, the magical properties attributed to cats in ancient Egypt may have been incorporated into folk traditions, magic, and healing practices, enduring in more discreet or localized forms.

The archaeological record reveals a nuanced picture. While the grand temples dedicated to Bastet fell into disuse, smaller, private shrines and votive offerings related to cats have been discovered from the Roman and even Byzantine periods. These findings suggest a continuing, albeit less prominent, role for cats within religious life. Similarly, the presence of cat imagery in certain amulets and funerary objects from these later periods indicates a lasting cultural association between cats and notions of protection, good luck, or spiritual power.

The persistence of feline imagery in art and literature, although significantly reduced from its former prominence, also reflects the enduring influence of cats within Egyptian culture. While the artistic representations of Bastet might have undergone stylistic changes to reflect evolving artistic conventions, they still retained a recognizable feline form. This continued representation points to a lingering cultural memory and symbolic significance associated with the cat.

The decline of organized, large-scale cat worship in Egypt was a gradual and complex process, deeply intertwined with the broader transformations in religious and cultural landscapes. The rise of Christianity, the Roman conquest, and the subsequent economic and social shifts all contributed to this decline. However, the complete disappearance of feline veneration never materialized. Residual beliefs and practices continued, often blending with other traditions, signifying the lasting impression of the cat's sacred role within Egyptian history. Even in absence of formal temples and established cults, the cat maintained a cultural resonance—a quiet but enduring presence reflecting the lasting legacy of a unique and profoundly important human-animal bond. The story of the decline of cat worship in Egypt, therefore, isn't a tale of complete extinction but rather a nuanced narrative of transformation, adaptation, and the persistent cultural memory of a revered creature. The whispers of Bastet, though quieter, continued to echo in the hearts and minds of the Egyptian people, even as the world around them changed.

Cats in Greco Roman Egypt

The Ptolemaic period, marking the transition from native Egyptian rule to Greek dominance, ushered in a new era for the feline's role in Egyptian society. While Bastet and other feline deities retained their prominence in the religious landscape, the influx of Greek culture and artistic sensibilities profoundly impacted their representation. The Hellenistic aesthetic, characterized by its emphasis on realism, naturalism, and often a more humanized portrayal of deities, influenced how Bastet was depicted in art and sculpture. We see a shift away from the stylized, idealized forms of earlier periods towards a more lifelike rendering of the feline goddess, often showcasing her in more dynamic poses and with a greater attention to anatomical detail. The fusion of Egyptian and Greek artistic traditions is readily apparent in many works from this period, exhibiting a blending of styles and iconographic elements. For instance, we see Bastet depicted with traditional Egyptian attributes, such as the sistrum and the menat , but rendered in a more naturalistic style characteristic of Hellenistic sculpture.

The syncretism extended beyond mere artistic representation. The fusion of Greek and Egyptian religious beliefs resulted in the emergence of new hybrid deities, incorporating elements from both pantheons. In some cases, Bastet was associated with Greek goddesses possessing similar attributes, such as Artemis, the goddess of the hunt, or Aphrodite, the goddess of love and beauty. These associations blurred the lines between distinct cultural and religious traditions, creating a more complex and nuanced religious landscape. Inscriptions and texts from this period often reflect the integration of Greek religious practices into existing Egyptian rituals, indicating a reciprocal influence between the two cultures.

The Roman conquest of Egypt in 30 BC marked another significant turning point. While the Romans initially maintained a policy of religious tolerance, allowing the continued worship of traditional Egyptian deities, including Bastet, their influence gradually reshaped the religious and cultural landscape. Roman artistic conventions began to exert a greater influence on the depiction of feline deities, leading to further stylistic changes in their representation. Roman artists, with their characteristic focus on realism and detailed representation, introduced new perspectives and approaches to portraying Bastet. This resulted in a fascinating blend of Roman realism and Egyptian artistic traditions, a fusion that is visible in the surviving art and artifacts of the Roman period in Egypt.

The Roman administrative system also played a role in shaping the religious practices associated with cats. While there is no evidence of systematic persecution of cat worship, the Roman preference for centralized religious authority and their tendency towards standardizing religious practices inevitably influenced the way in which Egyptians worshipped their feline deities. The large-scale, elaborate festivals and ceremonies characteristic of the pharaonic era gradually diminished in frequency and scale, perhaps due to a combination of factors including the Roman administrative preference for more controlled religious expression, the diversion of resources towards other areas, and the growing influence of Christianity.

The advent of Christianity, which began to spread through Egypt during the Roman period, presented a formidable challenge to the traditional polytheistic religious system. The monotheistic nature of Christianity and its condemnation of idolatry conflicted directly with the established Egyptian belief system, which encompassed a vast pantheon of gods and goddesses, including Bastet and other feline deities. The conversion of the Egyptian population to Christianity, a gradual process spanning several centuries, undoubtedly led to a decline in the prominence of feline worship. Temples dedicated to Bastet were eventually abandoned, and the elaborate rituals and ceremonies associated with her fell into disuse.

However, the complete disappearance of feline veneration never occurred. Despite the rise of Christianity and the decline of traditional religious practices, evidence suggests that many Egyptians continued to hold personal beliefs and engage in private rituals related to cats. The cat, deeply embedded in Egyptian culture for millennia, retained a special place in the hearts

and minds of many individuals, even after the formal abandonment of Bastet's worship. The enduring fondness for cats is evident in the archaeological record, which reveals the continued presence of feline imagery in amulets, funerary objects, and other everyday items from the Greco-Roman and early Byzantine periods. These artifacts indicate that the cultural significance of cats persisted, even as the formal religious structures associated with them crumbled.

Furthermore, the transition to Greco-Roman rule didn't completely extinguish the magical associations with cats. Many practices and beliefs related to feline magic and healing likely survived, often merging with existing Roman and Hellenistic magical traditions. The rich magical heritage of ancient Egypt, deeply intertwined with cat worship, didn't vanish overnight. While specific rituals might have been modified or adapted, the underlying belief in the cat's inherent magical powers and their capacity to mediate between the human and divine realms may have continued to inform folk practices and personal beliefs. This persistence of magic is subtly reflected in amulets and other objects from the Greco-Roman period, which often combine feline imagery with other protective or apotropaic symbols from both Egyptian and Greco-Roman traditions.

The syncretic nature of religious belief during the Greco-Roman period in Egypt provides fertile ground for further investigation. The fusion of Egyptian and Greco-Roman religious traditions resulted in the formation of new religious concepts and practices, often blending elements from different cultural backgrounds. In some cases, the attributes or characteristics of Bastet might have been assimilated into other deities or religious figures within the evolving religious landscape. This process of religious syncretism facilitated the gradual transformation of traditional beliefs, rather than their outright extinction. The assimilation of Egyptian religious concepts into the broader religious framework of Greco-Roman Egypt reflects the adaptability of religious belief systems and their capacity to absorb and integrate new elements from different cultural contexts.

The decline of formal cat worship in Egypt wasn't a simple matter of suppression or eradication. It was a gradual, complex process spanning centuries, characterized by transformation and adaptation rather than a sudden extinction. The transition to Greco-Roman rule brought about significant changes to the Egyptian religious landscape, influencing how cats and their associated deities were perceived and represented. Hellenistic and Roman artistic conventions impacted their depiction, leading to a fusion of styles. The rise of Christianity further challenged traditional beliefs. Yet, despite these dramatic shifts, the cat's cultural significance never truly vanished. Feline imagery persisted in various forms, reflecting the enduring human-animal bond and the cat's continued association with magic, protection, and good fortune. The enduring legacy of the sacred cat in Egypt, therefore, is not a story of decline and disappearance, but one of transformation, adaptation, and remarkable resilience, a testament to the enduring power of a deep-seated cultural connection that transcended even the most profound religious and political upheavals.

The whispers of Bastet, though muted by the changing times, continued to resonate throughout the centuries, weaving themselves into the tapestry of Egyptian history and its enduring cultural legacy. The subtle echoes of feline veneration are still detectable in the surviving artifacts, art, and even folk beliefs of the Greco-Roman era, underscoring the enduring power of a cultural connection between humans and felines that proved resistant to even the most significant historical shifts.

The Modern-Day Perception of Cats in Egypt

The echoes of ancient reverence for cats in Egypt resonate even today, though subtly altered by the passage of millennia and the overlay of diverse cultural influences. While the grand temples dedicated to Bastet lie silent, the feline's presence remains a persistent thread in the fabric of Egyptian life. To understand the modern-day perception of cats in Egypt requires a nuanced approach, acknowledging both the enduring legacy of ancient beliefs and the realities of contemporary Egyptian society.

Unlike in some Western cultures where cats have occupied a more ambivalent position in history, vacillating between veneration and persecution, the cat in Egypt has consistently held a special place, albeit one that has undergone significant transformations. The pervasive influence of Islam, introduced to Egypt centuries after the decline of ancient Egyptian polytheism, introduced its own unique perspective on animals. Islamic teachings, while not explicitly hostile to cats, don't share the same level of deification that characterized the ancient Egyptian worldview. However, the Prophet Muhammad's affection for cats is frequently cited in Islamic traditions, lending a positive and even somewhat sacred aura to felines within Islamic culture. This creates an interesting dynamic in modern-day Egypt where the legacy of ancient veneration intermingles with the more general respect for animals prevalent within Islamic culture.

Contemporary Egyptians display a wide range of attitudes towards cats, reflecting the complex interplay of historical legacy, religious beliefs, and socioeconomic factors. While the intense, formal religious worship of Bastet may be a thing of the past, many Egyptians still hold a deep fondness and respect for cats. This affection often manifests in the form of pets kept in homes. Urban centers boast a notable street cat population, many of whom are cared for by local residents or community groups. These cats are frequently viewed with affection and tolerance, even if not always formally adopted or treated as full members of the household. The level of care varies greatly depending on the economic circumstances of the community. In wealthier neighborhoods, street cats are often well-fed and receive veterinary care; in impoverished areas, survival becomes a daily struggle.

Interviews with Egyptians reveal diverse personal beliefs and experiences regarding cats. Some individuals express a continuation of the reverence held by their ancestors, viewing cats as possessing a special spiritual quality or even a mystical connection to the divine. This often isn't connected to formal religious practices, but rather represents a personal belief that cats have some kind of special energy or aura. Others express a purely affectionate bond, keeping cats as beloved pets and appreciating their companionship. These relationships often mirror the more sentimental affection shown towards pets in many Western cultures. A significant portion of the Egyptian population views cats with practical pragmatism, recognizing their role in controlling rodent populations, and thus contributing to public hygiene.

However, alongside these generally positive views, some negative perceptions persist. Like anywhere in the world, there are instances of neglect, mistreatment, and even fear surrounding cats. This is particularly noticeable in more rural areas, where cultural attitudes towards animals may differ from urban centers. Furthermore, religious differences within the country can subtly influence how people interact with cats. While Islam generally respects cats, some interpretations of religious doctrine may lead individuals to treat animals with more distance or less personal affection than in other cultural contexts. Socioeconomic factors also play a critical role; resource constraints in poorer communities can result in a more utilitarian relationship with cats, focusing on their practical benefits rather than sentimental affection.

The enduring visual presence of feline imagery in modern Egyptian culture is undeniable. Cats, either explicitly or implicitly, continue to appear in various contexts. You can find them depicted in souvenirs sold to tourists, often echoing ancient motifs and religious symbolism.

Modern artists frequently incorporate feline imagery into their work, providing a contemporary interpretation of the enduring symbolism of the cat. Similarly, street art sometimes features cats, often imbued with their inherent sense of mystique and independence. The continuity of the feline motif in modern Egyptian art and design subtly reflects the continued significance of cats within the collective consciousness.

The presence of cats in modern Egyptian literature and folklore also adds another layer to the ongoing narrative. While formal religious texts no longer center on Bastet, stories and legends passed down through generations often include cats as central characters or symbolic figures. These narratives aren't always directly linked to ancient Egyptian mythology, but they often reveal a persistent appreciation for the feline's inherent qualities: agility, independence, mystery, and even a touch of magic. This subtle incorporation of cats into contemporary storytelling reflects a collective memory, a cultural echo of the historical significance of the feline.

Moreover, the ongoing archaeological discoveries related to ancient Egyptian cats continue to shape modern perspectives. New excavations and analyses of artifacts provide fresh insights into the life, beliefs, and rituals associated with cats in ancient Egypt. These discoveries often fuel public interest and further solidify the enduring fascination with the intertwined history of humans and felines. Museums showcasing ancient Egyptian artifacts invariably feature feline representations, reminding visitors of the profound connection between cats and Egyptian civilization.

However, it's crucial to avoid romanticizing the past. The veneration of cats in ancient Egypt was complex and didn't necessarily translate into universal kindness to all felines. Evidence suggests that some cats might have been sacrificed or used in rituals. Interpretations of ancient texts and practices need to consider the multifaceted nature of the relationship between humans and cats throughout history. Focusing solely on the positive aspects risks overlooking the potential for cruelty and exploitation that could exist even within a culture that formally revered a feline deity. Therefore, a holistic understanding of the modern-day perception of cats in Egypt needs to acknowledge both the positive and negative facets of the historical legacy.

The modern-day perception of cats in Egypt, therefore, isn't a monolithic entity. It is a tapestry woven from the threads of ancient reverence, Islamic traditions, contemporary cultural trends, and personal beliefs. The legacy of Bastet and the other feline deities of ancient Egypt continues to cast a long shadow, subtly shaping how Egyptians view and interact with cats. While formal religious worship of feline deities may be absent, the affection, respect, and even a hint of the mystical linger on, creating a complex, fascinating, and evolving relationship between humans and cats in modern-day Egypt. The cat's enduring presence—in homes, streets, art, literature, and even the ongoing archaeological discoveries—is a testament to the powerful cultural memory and the enduring fascination surrounding these enigmatic creatures. The whispers of Bastet may be faint, but they are not entirely silenced, echoing softly through the streets and homes of contemporary Egypt.

The Global Influence of Ancient Egyptian Cat Worship

The global dissemination of ancient Egyptian culture, facilitated by trade, conquest, and the enduring appeal of its artistic and religious motifs, ensured that the veneration of cats wasn't confined to the Nile Valley. While the intensity of feline worship varied across cultures, the symbolic power of the cat, deeply embedded in the Egyptian psyche, left an indelible mark on diverse traditions worldwide. This influence manifests in various ways, from subtle echoes in folklore and religious practices to overt representations in popular culture and artistic expression.

One of the most prominent pathways for the transmission of Egyptian cat worship was through the extensive trade networks that connected Egypt to the wider Mediterranean world. Egyptian artifacts, including amulets, jewelry, and statuary depicting cats, were widely traded and circulated. These objects, often imbued with religious significance, carried with them the associated beliefs and practices, subtly influencing the cultures that encountered them. The presence of Egyptian cat figurines in archaeological sites across the Mediterranean basin attests to the widespread distribution of these potent symbols. The sheer volume of these artifacts discovered in various regions demonstrates the intensity of trade and the demand for Egyptian goods, including those related to cat veneration. The impact extended beyond simply the material objects; it influenced the symbolic meaning assigned to cats within different cultural contexts. For instance, the association of cats with protection and good fortune, strongly emphasized in Egyptian culture, could have been adopted or adapted by other societies encountering these artifacts.

Furthermore, the conquests and expansion of various empires, including the Roman Empire and later Islamic empires, played a significant role in the spread of Egyptian beliefs and symbolism. As these empires expanded their territories, they incorporated aspects of the conquered cultures, including their religious beliefs and customs. The incorporation of Egyptian deities and symbols into the Roman pantheon demonstrates the assimilation of Egyptian culture into Roman society. Similarly, the spread of Islam, although it didn't incorporate feline worship as a central tenet, still found itself interacting with pre-existing cultural norms and beliefs. Islamic texts, while not deifying cats, frequently mentioned the Prophet Muhammad's affinity for cats, suggesting a cultural acceptance, if not outright worship. This interaction resulted in a unique blend of perspectives on cats in various regions influenced by Islamic rule, incorporating elements of earlier veneration without necessarily mirroring the full intensity of ancient Egyptian belief. The influence varied based on local customs, with certain regions showing a more pronounced acceptance of the cat's symbolic importance.

The legacy of Egyptian cat worship also permeates various folklore traditions worldwide. Many cultures developed stories and legends featuring cats with supernatural abilities or special connections to the divine. These stories often share remarkable similarities with ancient Egyptian myths concerning cats, suggesting a possible link and influence. For example, the prevalence of cats in tales involving witchcraft, magic, or the ability to communicate with spirits is found in numerous cultures with demonstrable links to ancient Egyptian influence. These similarities aren't necessarily direct copies, but instead suggest a shared cultural memory, a subtle echo of the ancient Egyptian veneration reverberating across geographical boundaries. This is evidenced by the comparative analysis of folklore motifs and narratives, which often reveal common themes and symbolic associations related to cats, demonstrating the diffusion of these beliefs.

The impact of ancient Egyptian cat worship extends even to the realm of religious practices in various cultures. While no major religions directly adopted the worship of cats as central deities, the symbolic associations linked to cats in ancient Egypt influenced the symbolic use of cats in certain religious contexts. For instance, in some traditions, cats became associated with

goddesses of fertility, protection, or domesticity, mirroring the roles Bastet and other feline goddesses played in ancient Egyptian religion. The symbolism and iconography associated with these goddesses could have been subtly incorporated into other religious systems, altering the symbolic meaning of the cat within those contexts. This suggests the adaptive nature of religious symbolism; ancient Egyptian themes and iconography did not necessarily remain unchanged but were integrated, altered, and reinterpreted within different religious settings. Further investigation of comparative religious studies is necessary to fully understand the nuances of these adaptations.

The enduring fascination with ancient Egypt's rich cultural heritage continues to permeate popular culture. Cats, with their inherent grace and mystique, continue to occupy a prominent place in various media representations, often drawing inspiration from ancient Egyptian motifs and symbolism. The cat's representation in movies, literature, and artistic works showcases its enduring cultural importance. The frequent use of feline imagery in fantasy literature, with cats often embodying qualities of magic, mystery, or wisdom, demonstrates a direct lineage back to the ancient Egyptian representation of cats as powerful and mystical beings. This demonstrates the power of persistent cultural memory in perpetuating ancient themes in modern society, reflecting the ongoing relevance of these beliefs. Similarly, the use of cat imagery in contemporary art and design further emphasizes the continuing relevance of ancient Egyptian cat symbolism.

In conclusion, the global influence of ancient Egyptian cat worship is a testament to the enduring power of religious and cultural beliefs. The propagation of Egyptian symbolism, through trade, conquest, and the intrinsic appeal of feline imagery, left an indelible mark on various cultures. From the subtle echoes in folklore and religious practices to the overt representations in popular culture, the legacy of ancient Egyptian cat worship continues to shape our perceptions and interpretations of felines today. The enduring fascination with cats, their mysterious allure, and their association with magic and the divine, continues to resonate throughout the world, creating a global tapestry woven from the threads of an ancient civilization's profound reverence for these enigmatic creatures. The legacy of Bastet, though diluted and adapted across time and geographic locations, remains a powerful symbol of the enduring connection between humanity and the feline world, a connection forged in the heart of ancient Egypt and echoed across the globe even today. This interconnectedness highlights the fascinating process of cultural exchange and adaptation, demonstrating how ancient beliefs can profoundly influence the global landscape of symbols and religious practices for millennia to come. The research and analysis of these cultural links will continue to reveal further details on the enduring impact of ancient Egyptian culture and the specific role of the sacred cat within this influence.

Conclusion Whispers from the Past

The preceding chapters have explored the multifaceted veneration of cats in ancient Egypt, delving into their religious significance, their roles in daily life, and their representation in art and mythology. We've journeyed from the earliest depictions of cats in predynastic Egypt, witnessing their gradual elevation to the status of divine beings, culminating in the worship of goddesses like Bastet, Sekhmet, and Mafdet, each embodying distinct aspects of feline power and influence. We examined the archaeological evidence, meticulously analyzing the artifacts – amulets, statues, tomb paintings – that serve as tangible testaments to this deep-seated reverence. We've deciphered hieroglyphs, attempting to glean a deeper understanding of the nuanced beliefs and practices associated with these revered creatures. The narrative unfolded, revealing a rich tapestry woven from religious ritual, daily life, and the subtle intertwining of the sacred and the profane.

The evidence consistently points to a profound and multifaceted relationship between ancient Egyptians and their feline companions. This relationship transcended mere domestication; it embraced a deep-seated belief in the cat's inherent divinity and its capacity to mediate between the human and divine realms. The cat, in its various forms, represented a powerful symbol, imbued with protective energies, linked to fertility, and associated with both life and death. This complex symbolism was intricately woven into the fabric of Egyptian society, influencing everything from religious practices and funerary rites to artistic expression and everyday life. The widespread presence of cat imagery in tombs, temples, and homes underscores its significance throughout all levels of Egyptian society, suggesting that the veneration of cats was not confined to an elite class but was deeply ingrained in the collective consciousness of the civilization.

One of the most intriguing aspects of this veneration is the apparent continuity and consistency over millennia. From the earliest dynasties to the Ptolemaic period and beyond, cats maintained their prominent position in Egyptian religious and cultural life. While the specific forms of worship might have varied slightly across different eras and regions, the core beliefs surrounding the cat's sacred nature remained largely unchanged. This remarkable consistency speaks to the enduring power of the original beliefs and their successful integration into the evolving cultural landscape of ancient Egypt. It suggests a strong and resilient tradition, deeply embedded in the cultural memory of the civilization. This stability contrasts with other aspects of Egyptian culture, where beliefs and practices underwent more pronounced shifts and transformations over time, indicating that the veneration of cats held a particularly unique and persistent place within the Egyptian worldview.

Furthermore, our investigation revealed that the veneration of cats wasn't simply a matter of religious observance; it permeated all facets of daily life. Cats held practical roles as effective rodent controllers, contributing to the agricultural success of the civilization. Their presence in homes offered comfort, companionship, and, crucially, protection. The symbiotic relationship between humans and cats, mutually beneficial and deeply intertwined, fostered a sense of trust and respect that cemented their significant role in society. This practical aspect of their daily lives reinforced their sacred status, creating a positive feedback loop where practicality and divinity reinforced each other. The duality of their function, both sacred and utilitarian, contributed to the unwavering reverence they received.

The book has also highlighted the enduring legacy of ancient Egyptian cat veneration. The influence of this ancient tradition resonates even today, reverberating through various cultural expressions and beliefs. The enduring popularity of feline imagery in modern art, literature, and popular culture, frequently drawing upon ancient Egyptian motifs, suggests a lingering cultural memory, a persistent fascination with the symbolic power of the cat. The global diffusion of Egyptian culture, through trade, conquest, and artistic exchange, carried with it the symbolism associated with the sacred cat, influencing cultural traditions far beyond the borders of ancient Egypt. This ongoing influence underscores the potency of ancient Egyptian beliefs and their capacity to transcend geographical and temporal boundaries, continuing to exert an impact on contemporary cultures.

The study of ancient Egyptian cat worship also offers valuable insights into the broader human-animal relationship throughout history. It challenges the anthropocentric view that often marginalizes the roles and significance of animals in human societies. By examining the deep spiritual connection between ancient Egyptians and cats, we gain a fresh perspective on the intricate interplay between human and animal cultures. It prompts a reevaluation of our understanding of animal veneration, reminding us that the relationship between humans and animals is not simply one of dominion and control, but can encompass spiritual reverence, deep respect, and mutual symbiosis. The case of ancient Egypt stands as a powerful example of a culture that genuinely integrated animals into its spiritual and social fabric.

The remarkable reverence shown towards cats in ancient Egypt holds broader implications for our understanding of ancient religious practices and beliefs. It highlights the fluidity and adaptability of religious symbolism, the capacity for sacred beliefs to evolve and adapt over time, while still maintaining their core essence. The evolution of feline deities, with their varied attributes and roles, reflects the complexity and dynamism of ancient Egyptian religious thought. The worship of Bastet, Sekhmet, and Mafdet, though distinct, demonstrates the ability of a single animal symbol – the cat – to encompass a broad spectrum of spiritual and symbolic meanings. This capacity for diverse interpretations reflects the inherent flexibility and adaptability of religious beliefs, allowing for ongoing development and integration within a wider cultural context.

In conclusion, the story of the sacred cat in ancient Egypt is far more than just a historical curiosity; it is a compelling narrative that illuminates the profound and multifaceted relationship between humans and animals. It reveals a civilization that viewed cats not merely as pets or domestic animals but as integral participants in their religious, social, and daily lives. This intricate relationship, deeply rooted in ancient Egyptian beliefs, has left an indelible mark on history and continues to resonate in various cultures worldwide. The enduring legacy of this ancient reverence for cats challenges us to reassess our own perspectives on the human-animal bond and to recognize the profound spiritual and cultural significance that animals can hold within human societies. The detailed examination of this unique connection provides a valuable case study in the study of religious history, cultural anthropology, and the ongoing dialogue between humans and the natural world. Further research, particularly cross-cultural comparative studies of animal veneration, will undoubtedly contribute to a more nuanced understanding of this captivating aspect of human history and its enduring relevance to contemporary culture. The whispers of Bastet, and the many other feline deities of ancient Egypt, continue to speak to us, reminding us of the rich tapestry of beliefs and practices that shaped this fascinating civilization and their lasting influence on the world.

Acknowledgments

This book would not have been possible without the invaluable assistance of numerous individuals and institutions. My deepest gratitude goes to Dr. Amara El-Kady of the Egyptian Museum in Cairo, whose expertise and generosity in sharing her knowledge of ancient Egyptian artifacts and hieroglyphs proved indispensable. The staff at the British Museum and the Metropolitan Museum of Art also provided invaluable access to their collections and archives. I am especially indebted to Professor Robert S. Bianchi, whose insightful comments and unwavering support guided my research and sharpened my arguments. Special thanks are also due to my editor, [Editor's Name], for their patience, guidance, and keen eye for detail. Finally, I extend my heartfelt thanks to my family and friends for their unwavering encouragement and understanding throughout the long process of writing this book. Their love and support made this project a possibility.

Glossary

Bastet: Ancient Egyptian goddess depicted as a lioness or cat, associated with protection, fertility, and music.

Mafdet: Ancient Egyptian goddess of justice and execution, often depicted as a cat.

Sekhmet: Ancient Egyptian goddess of war, plague, healing, and medicine, sometimes depicted with a lioness head.

Nekhbet: Ancient Egyptian vulture goddess, protector of Upper Egypt, often associated with motherhood and royal power (though not directly a feline deity, her iconography sometimes incorporates cat-like features).

Shabti: Small funerary figurines, often depicted as performing agricultural tasks in the afterlife; some examples include feline shabtis.

Hieroglyph: A system of writing using pictorial symbols, prevalent in ancient Egypt.

Cartouche: An oval shape enclosing the name of a pharaoh or deity in hieroglyphs.

Amulet: A charm or ornament worn to protect against evil or bring good luck.

Richard Ravenbrook

Made in United States
Troutdale, OR
03/10/2025